I0092757

GOLDEN PAWS AT SUNSET BEACH

Golden Paws Legacy, Book 1

Written by Diane Kann

Illustrated by

Gennell Grefaldo and Mary Grace Victoria

Kannceptual Creations

Paws to Read

A moment shared is a memory made.

Visit us at: *boltandcharliebooks.com*

© 2025 Diane Kann

All rights reserved.

No part of this publication may be reproduced, stored in a retrieval system, or transmitted in any form or by any means—electronic, mechanical, photocopying, recording, or otherwise—without prior written permission of the publisher, except in the case of brief quotations for review or educational use.

Published by Kannceptual Creations LLC

An imprint of Bolt and Charlie Books

boltandcharliebooks.com

Illustrations by Gennell Grefaldo and Mary Grace Victoria

ISBN: 978-1-969569-15-9

Printed in the United States of America

First Edition, October 2025

Paws to Read is a Bolt and Charlie Books initiative promoting early literacy and shared storytime experiences.

TABLE OF CONTENTS

DEDICATION

For the guardians of the shore— the silent watchers who keep the balance between sea and sand, the brave creatures who follow the moonlight into the waves, and the dreamers who feel the ocean's call in their hearts.

May you always have the courage to stand watch when it matters, to walk gently where life begins, and to remember that even the smallest act of care can ripple outward like waves across the sea.

This is for the turtles who return home to begin again, for the guardians who keep them safe, and for you— because the world is waiting for the light only you can bring.

Chapter 1
THE DOG AND THE DARK WATER

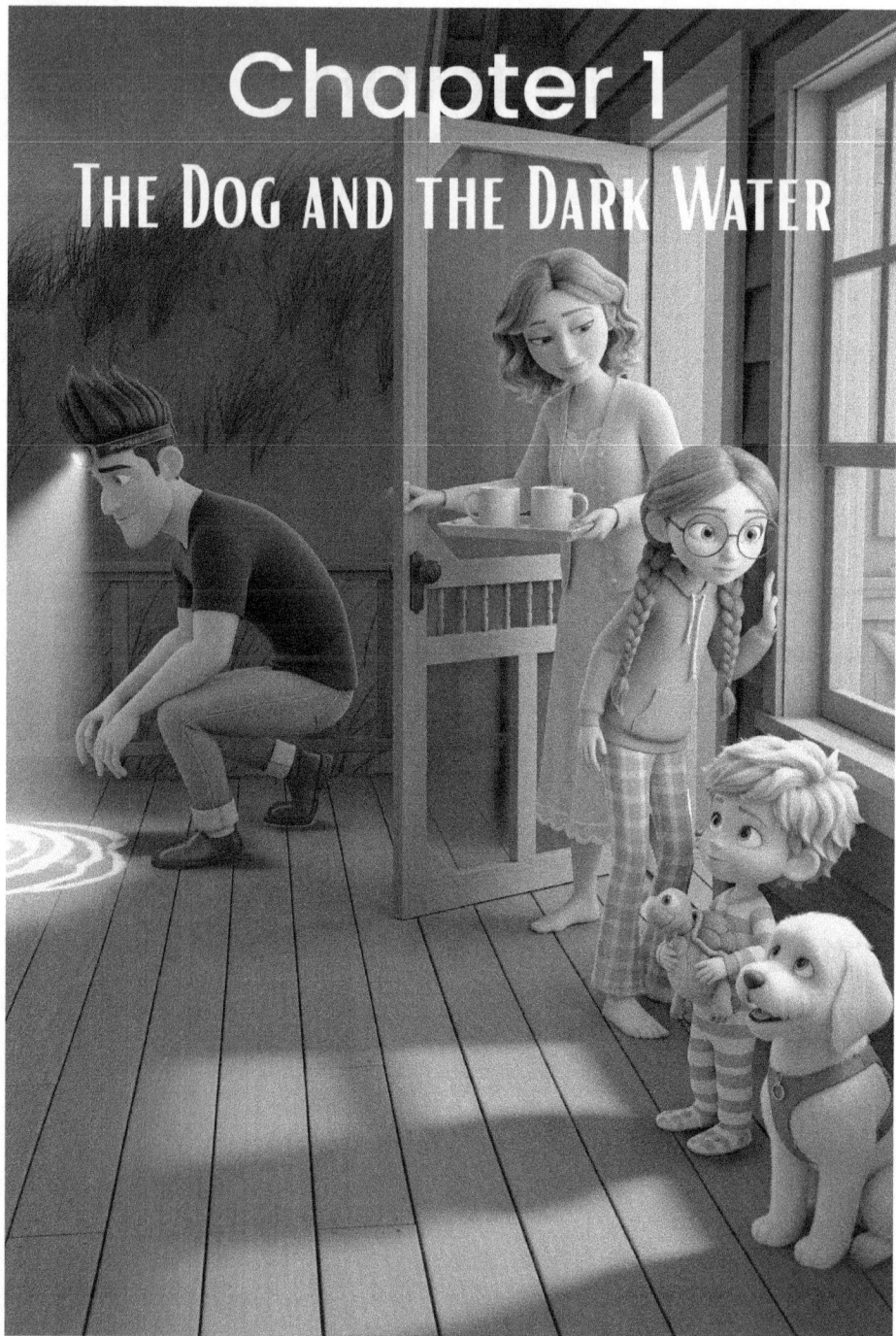

The night settled soft over Sunset Beach, the surf breathing in long, even strokes like something great and living had fallen asleep alongside the shore. A single halogen bulb washed the Reynolds' back steps in weak gold, catching a coil of line, a dented bucket, and the shadows of dune grass bowing to the breeze. Farther out, the ocean stitched and unstitched the seam of sand with its patient hush.

Sarah nudged the screen door with a hip and stepped onto the porch with a tray of mugs. "Tea," she called, because naming comfort was sometimes a way to make it real.

Mark didn't answer. His headlamp made a moving coin on the beach as he crouched at the tideline, gloved fingers testing a ribbon of black that had not been there yesterday. The smell that lifted was wrong—solvent riding the brine, a metallic echo beneath the honest salt. For a week he'd told himself the skim of milk-white near shore was just a spring churn. Tonight the sea had written in ink.

A small white form slipped under the rail and paused beside Sarah's ankle, nose lifted. Paws—thirty pounds of Eskie-Doodle with a plume tail and snowbright curls freckled by sand—snuffed the air once, then again, sharper. He gave a soft, contained chuff and tapped one front paw on the porch plank: tap, sit—his alert, practiced in the shelter's obedience class and reinforced in Sophie's careful hands every morning since.

Sophie was already at the glass, tracking the lighthouse sweep across her palm. "He's alerting," she whispered, excitement and unease braided tight. "Can I go out? I'll leash him."

"Shoes, jacket," Sarah said, automatic as breath. She reached down; Paws leaned into the slip of his harness, tag tink-tinking—a little fish they'd let Leo pick the day they brought him home from Bayshore Shelter. Two months in, he still wore a look of formal gratitude whenever a hand touched the buckle, as if adoption were a contract he intended to honor.

On the sand, the dog's paws made small, neat dimples beside Mark's boot prints. He lowered his head toward the black thread drawn along the wrack line and snorted, then sat again, ears pricked. Tap, sit.

"Good boy," Mark murmured, eyes on the stain. "We hear you."

Sarah came down the steps with Sophie and Leo in tow—Sophie steady with the leash, Leo clutching his stuffed turtle like a talisman. The wind shifted and carried the wrongness inland, a headachy top note that made Sarah's jaw tighten. "That isn't kelp," she said.

"It isn't," Mark agreed. He swept his lamp north. The ribbon feathered, pooled heavier in low pockets, clung in pepper flecks to the ripple marks. "And it's fresh."

Sophie's hand found Paws' ruff. He settled against her shin, eyes bright, tail tip beating once, twice. His adoption had been a quiet miracle: a shelter card that read "friendly, eager, likes puzzles," a staffer's hopeful smile, the boy with the fish tag, a family photo taken in a hallway that smelled of bleach and beginnings. He had learned their rhythms fast—morning runs, porch naps, a gentle obsession with retrieving lost socks—and, more recently, how to touch his paw to Sophie's boot when he scented what they'd started to call the "bad water."

Mark pulled out his phone and scrolled to a name he hadn't expected to need so often. "Ranger Hayes? Mark Reynolds on Gull. We've got a petroleum-type residue. A few hundred yards at least. High viscosity, tacky. Not algae."

"Copy, Mr. Reynolds," came the reply, voice steady and pre-dawn calm. "Hold your position; don't handle product. We'll roll a tech. If it's pooling, we'll try to boom Heron's on the low. You near the inlet?"

"Half a mile south," Mark said.

"We're twenty out. Keep kids and—" Hayes paused, as if picking up the faint jingle through the phone "—pets off the wet. We'll bring pads if it's heavy."

"Roger."

Sophie knelt. Paws' ears tipped to her voice. "You're working, but we're staying on the dry, okay?" He licked the back of her hand like an oath.

The ranger truck nosed up Gull Road with strobes dimmed to a hush of blue. The porch became a little room of light while the beach beyond held its dark counsel. Paws lay sphinx-still by the steps, harness on, leash looped in Sophie's fingers; his body hummed with the effort of not going where his nose wanted.

Ranger David Hayes swung down with the contained urgency of a man who knew panic wasted time. Officer Anya Sharma followed with a hard case and the focused economy that made every motion count. Introductions were a blur of names and nods; the ocean kept breathing.

"This your line?" Hayes asked, chin angling toward the stain.

"Started down by the drift fence, now up toward the creek," Mark said. "We didn't go past the cut."

Anya knelt. Under the bite of her headlamp the smear became a thing with map and margin. She set a scale card, drew off a sheen into a glass jar, scraped tacky residue into a vial, labeled quick, clean letters. "Clingy," she said. "You're right about viscosity. Waste blend, most likely. Not a simple fuel slick."

"Origin?" Hayes asked.

"Small craft, mid-tide, nozzle discharge," she said, eyes tracing the way flecks had jumped higher on windward grit. "They hugged the bar. No roll marks from containers."

Hayes' radio hissed to life. "Boom team rolling. Thirty minutes on the low."

He lifted his gaze to the family. It snagged on the dog and warmed by a degree. "And who's your new deputy?"

"This is Paws," Sophie said, like a proper introduction. "We adopted him. He's an Eskie-Doodle. He alerts with his paw when he smells the bad water." Pride and worry pulled her words tight.

"Good nose," Hayes said, offering the back of his hand. Paws sniffed politely, then thumped his plume tail once. "Good choice," he added to the adults. "Shelter dogs are all heart."

Anya's glance flicked to the harness and tag; she smiled with her eyes. "Nice fit. If he had a chip, the shelter will have you on file anyway."

"He's ours," Sophie said, small and fierce.

They moved together along the line, the headlamps bobbing like slow fireflies. Anya read the shore the way a paramedic reads a face: where the stain had pooled in tufted sand, where the spray had freckled higher, where the wrack that should have caught the worst was oddly clean. "They know this shoreline," she said. "They picked the hour for cover and current. It isn't amateur."

"What do we do?" Sarah asked, jaw set against the smell.

"Tonight we contain what we can," Hayes said. "Tomorrow we see what we're up against."

The boom truck's beacon smeared orange against the dunes. In the wash of portable lights, the cove showed its shape: the inlet mouth like a waiting throat, the slow backdrift that could slip toxins into the marsh if left unguarded. The crew unfurled bright rolls across the black glass—anchors set, lines paid out, skimmers poised—a floating parenthesis to keep harm from swallowing itself into the reeds.

On the porch steps, Leo slid into Sarah's lap and surrendered to sleep, stuffed turtle mashed under his chin. Sophie kept one palm against Paws' shoulder, feeling the steady thrum of his breath. "Is it bad?" she asked, not looking away.

"It isn't good," Anya answered without trimming the truth. "But you called early. That helps."

Hayes spoke with the boom captain, radio murmuring. When he came back his attention was all for the family. "We'll have crews at first light," he said. "I'll swing by myself around sunup. In the meantime, keep him leashed if you're near the wet. That stuff will ride a coat and a paw pad for miles."

"We will," Sarah said.

Hayes hesitated. "Mind if I ask about traffic? Anything off in the last week? A truck idling at odd hours, skiffs running dark."

Sarah pictured the silver pickup that had paused at the road end three nights running, plates smeared in mud, dome light never coming on. "There's been a truck. It leaves when we walk toward it."

Mark nodded. "And a skiff outside the line two nights ago. No lights. We saw its wake more than the boat."

Hayes filed both away with a small motion of his mouth. "If they're dumping, they're scouting. Call in every odd thing. You don't have to decide what matters; that's on us." He looked pointedly at the rocks by the cut. "And don't let curiosity pull you toward the inlet. The current there doesn't care how careful you are."

"I won't," Sophie said, solemn as a lighthouse.

Paws lifted his paw and touched it to her boot. Tap. He did not whine. He did not pull. He had learned, quickly, the quiet between warning and worry.

Lights worked the cove until the ocean's patience demanded the low be kept. The ribbon of black dulled to brown where pads tangled it; a skimmer mumbled and hummed; the breeze turned and, for a blessed moment, the smell thinned to plain, clean salt.

Inside, Mark rinsed grit from his palms and stared into the sink as if water held answers. The house had been bought for its simple grace—a porch that held the day, a square of kitchen where steam made the windows fog, a back door that opened directly to sand. Tonight it felt like a watchpost.

"He's the best decision we've made in a long time," Sarah said quietly behind him.

Mark turned. Paws had arranged himself on the kitchen mat in a tidy curl, one paw tucked, tail cresting his flank, eyes half-closed but listening. He looked different in lamplight than he had in the shelter photo—fuller through the ribs, a coat gone from dull to luminous, the same attentive set to his ears. Sophie sat cross-legged beside him, tracing the fish tag with a finger.

"I think he knows he's home," Mark said.

Sophie didn't look up. "I think he knows we're his job."

They made up the pull-out for Leo with extra quilts. They tied a knot in the trash bag and set it outside. They put an old towel by the door for shoes. Mundane rituals, the sort that borrow a little order back from disorder.

Close to dawn, when the world felt fragile and new at once, Hayes' truck eased back up the lane. The boom still floated, gentle and stubborn. An egret stood knee-deep on the marsh edge like a sliver of moon.

"Morning," he said softly. His eyes were rimmed by what the night had cost. "Our lab's on call. We'll know more by noon."

"Do you think it's local?" Mark asked.

"I think somebody thinks Sunset is small enough not to notice," Hayes said. "I also think they're wrong."

Anya stepped around him with a new case and a tired smile for Sophie. "Your deputy kept it together," she said, nodding at Paws. "If you ever want to try a scent-games class, the shelter runs one on Saturdays.

It's fun, and it gives him a job that isn't just worrying about grown-ups."

"We'll be there," Sophie said, already decided.

Hayes took in the four of them, the dog, the porch, the beach. "You called," he said simply. "That's the difference between a mess and a case."

He tipped two fingers in a small salute and went back to the work that makes days safer for people who never know their names. The tide turned. The first honest light lifted the gray off the water and laid a thin blush over the sand, like the beach had decided to believe in morning again.

Paws stood and shook—soft bells of his tag, halo of salt mist, small body resetting itself for whatever came next. He nosed Sophie's palm, then went to the door and sat, plume tail sweeping once, twice, waiting for the day's orders.

"Breakfast," Sarah said, because love sometimes needs to be ordinary and immediate. "Then we'll see what the ocean tells us."

Out beyond the boom, the inlet gathered its secrets and tested the line. On the porch, a small dog in a red harness blinked at the new light and held still long enough to be leashed. And inside a house that had been built for weather and work and wonder, a family added one more ritual to the set that would come to define them: when the shore speaks, listen; when it flinches, move; when it hurts, call; and always, always, keep a hand on the heartbeat at your feet.

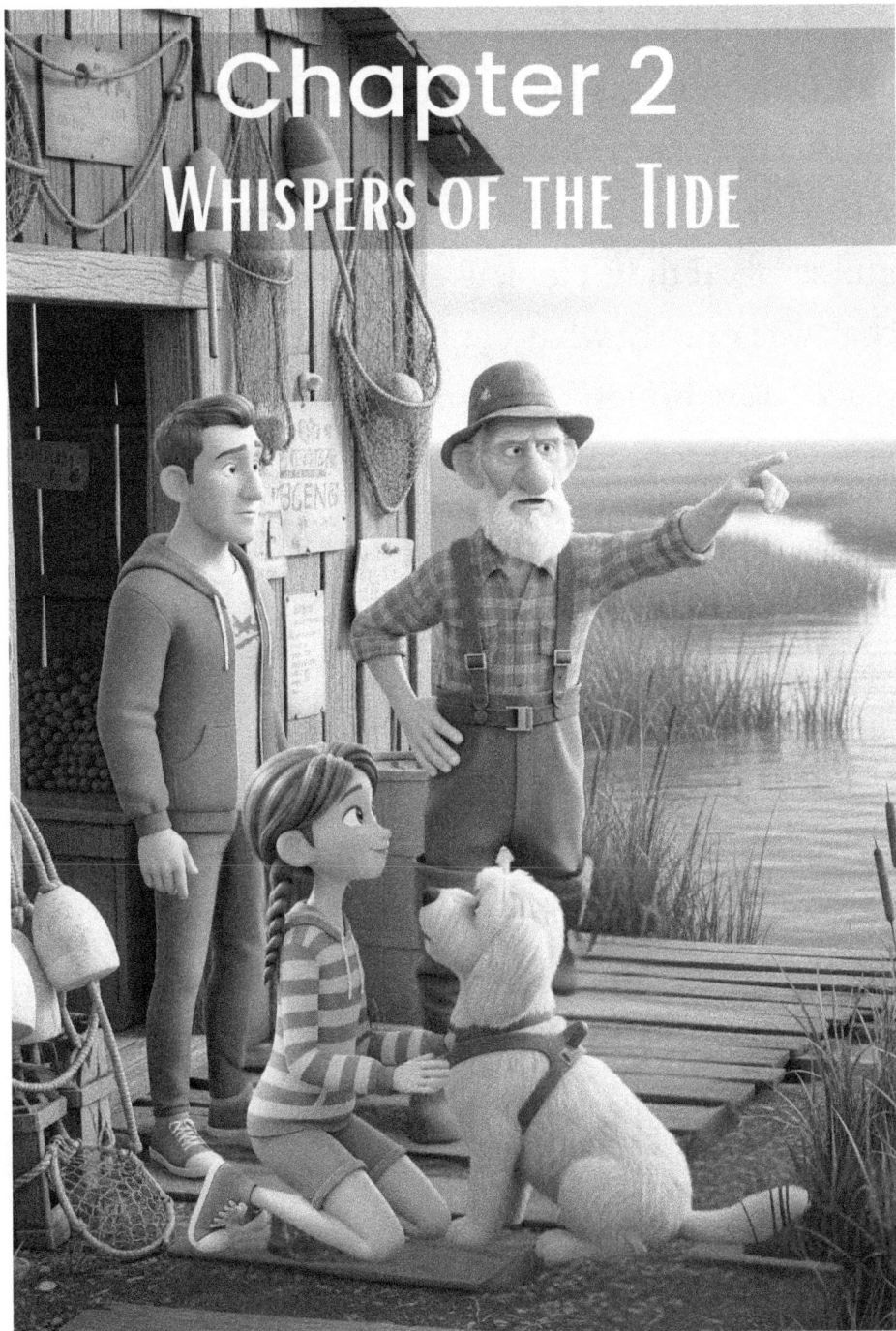

Chapter 2
WHISPERS OF THE TIDE

The first week at Sunset Beach slid by in a blur of salt and small introductions. The cottage—two bedrooms, a slouching porch, windows that rattled when the wind turned—sat on a thin rise of dune grass and scrub. It didn't look like much from the road, and that was exactly what Sarah loved about it. Modest places were honest. They made promises they could keep.

Mark took the attic for his desk—a door on two sawhorses, a secondhand chair that tilted left, and a view of the water he pretended didn't distract him. The consultancy work that was supposed to be steady had thinned to "we'll circle back," and he wore that fact like a shirt that didn't fit yet. Leo found the few flat patches of sand where his toy trucks didn't tip, and Sophie found the tide pools. Paws found everything.

He moved through the house like a rumor of golden light, nails clicking, nose working. If a cabinet was left ajar, he closed it with his hip. If a screen door latched poorly, he nosed it twice and then sat, pointedly, until someone fixed it. He learned the distances: the new back steps (three), the dune path (fifty-four), the cutoff to the beach (one hundred twenty-nine if you followed Leo's zigzags, ninety-seven if you walked like a person who didn't collect every shell).

On their second morning, the air carried a faint metallic tang beneath the usual brine. It wasn't strong. It was the kind of smell you only notice if you know a place well or if, like Paws, you notice everything.

He stopped at the edge of the tideline and lifted his head. The wind came in cool and steady from the southeast. He sniffed, sneezed once, and gave a low sound that wasn't a growl and wasn't quite a whine—more like a question pressed under his breath.

"What is it?" Sophie asked, already kneeling to stroke the ruff behind his ears. She was eleven—old enough to run ahead, young enough to report back every important discovery like it was a law. Paws leaned into her hand and then set his nose to the wet sand, tracing a lazy S as if following an invisible seam.

Mark squinted at the shallows. A dark sheen wavered across a narrow swath parallel to shore, no more than the width of a car. It broke and reformed with each wave, a skin on a skin.

"Algae?" he said, because sometimes it was just algae and it was important to remember that.

Sarah crouched and dipped a jar into the wash. "Algae doesn't usually smell like a toolbox," she murmured, capping the sample. "Or stick to your fingers like that."

They could have called it a fluke and gone home. Instead, Sarah labeled the jar with a date and a tide and a tiny star she used next to things that made her uneasy. Old habit from her years in the hospital. When something didn't sit right, you wrote it down and you checked again later. If it sat wrong twice, you told someone.

They told Ranger Anya Sharma, who arrived in a county pickup with mud on the tires and kindness under the brim of her hat. She carried a field kit that looked like a magician's suitcase and made time for Sophie's tide-pool tour even as she took notes.

"Could be runoff from up the coast," she said, drawing a second sample and setting a dab onto a strip that blushed at the edges. "Storm drain outfalls are tricky after a dry spell; first flush pulls all the summer dust with it. But... yeah, I smell it."

She didn't say *chemical*. She didn't have to. Paws, who had been content to lie under Sophie's hand, shifted closer to Sharma and sniffed the cuff of her sleeve. The ranger gave him a scratch like you'd sign a contract: deliberate, full attention.

"You folks new?" she asked.

"Three days," Sarah said. "We're from inland. Needed to—"

"—see the horizon," Mark finished.

Sharma smiled as if she knew exactly what it felt like to need more sky. "Welcome. If you notice that tang again, call the station. Better to over-report. And if you walk at night, red flashlight filters only on the beach; hatch season's overlapping this month." She handed them a card—**Turtle Lighting Guidelines** on one side, **Report Suspicious Activity** on the other—and met Sarah's eyes. "You won't be a bother."

They were not the only new things on the beach. In the evenings, a low hum threaded the horizon—a working boat's engine, maybe, or a generator farther out than you'd expect. It was easy to fold the sound into the ocean's own respiration and call it harmless. It was harder when Paws heard it, too. His ears flicked toward the dark water, and he did that breathy, held-back sound again, the one that lived somewhere between curiosity and caution.

"Probably a shrimp trawler," Mark said, watching for lights that didn't come. "Probably."

"Probably doesn't wag its tail like that," Leo announced, pointing. Paws' tail had crept down to half-mast, the way it did when he wanted to go forward but wasn't sure where the ground ended.

They trained him into a silent code because training was control, and control meant less fear when the world got loud. A tap at his shoulder meant *not now*. An open palm meant *show me*. A shhh, breath only, meant *stay* when *stay* would be too much sound. Paws learned fast because he liked being understood.

On the fourth night, the smell returned, thinner than before but stranger for it. A line of dead anchovies wrinkled the edge of the surf—nothing dramatic, just enough to turn gulls into a quick, white argument.

"Dead fish happen," Mr. Henderson said at the market the next morning, leaning more weight onto his cane when the linoleum squeaked. He had the kind of voice that lived comfortably at the end of a dock: carved by weather, never rushed. "Happened when I was a boy. Happens now. Question is whether it happens here or got washed in from away."

"Away," Sarah repeated, filing the word. It was big enough to be anywhere and small enough to be next door.

Henderson had a way of looking at you like he was reading tides on your forehead. "You the ones called Sharma about the sheen? Good. Keep calling. She's one of the ones who'll listen. You want the other one who listens, you find Silas."

He wrote a number on the back of a tourist map and circled a cove inland of the point where the marsh fingered down. "He sells bait out his shed and knows every sandbar that thinks it's a joke. Don't go in at low tide unless you want to leave your shoes."

They met Silas that afternoon—leathery hands, squint like a permanent question mark, a boat named **Perseverance** he'd re-lettered himself when the old paint failed. He took Paws' measure without making a ceremony out of it, like you'd glance at a sky and decide whether to hang laundry.

"You hear it?" he asked, chin up toward the open water.

"The hum?" Mark said.

"Mm." Silas hooked a thumb into his belt. "Not one of ours. Comes, goes. Running dark most nights. Stays well out past where common sense keeps decent people."

"You think it's—"

"I think people who don't want seeing don't get seen." He shifted his weight, then nodded at the channel that cut like a grin through the spit of sand. "Serpent's Tongue. You'll hear about it. You'll hear it, too, if the tide's against you. Rocks there wear their sharp outside. Little boats that try to slip in there after midnight sometimes forget what they are. You want to talk to the Coast Guard about that hum, you go ahead. They'll make notes. The hum will keep humming. Best thing is eyes on shore."

It wasn't a warning, not exactly. It was a neighbor handing you a light and trusting you not to set your own porch on fire.

The first community meeting was held in the back of the bakery, where the air tasted like cinnamon and flour and politics. A hand-lettered sign by the coffee urn read **TURTLES NEED THE DARK LIKE WE NEED SLEEP.** Someone had drawn a turtle with a cape. Someone else had added a speech bubble that said **NO CAPES** in a different ink.

The agenda looked harmless: beach lighting ordinance, voluntary trash pack-out, "quiet hours" on the dune paths. The argument started six minutes in.

"It's not fair to expect my guests to fumble around in the dark," said a man with a polo shirt that had a logo and a voice that had a microphone somewhere in its past. He ran a rental venue two blocks off the sand and had already used the word *destination* twice. "We pay taxes. We need to keep the area attractive and safe."

"Red bulbs are attractive," Mrs. Gable said from behind a tray of blueberry muffins. "They're practically fashion at this point."

"I'm not talking about... vibes," Polo Shirt said, and half the room sighed. "We lost a booking last spring because the bride's grandmother tripped on the path."

"Did she trip over the *light*?" Sarah asked, polite as sugar and impossible to ignore. "Or over an empty beer can in the path?"

There was a murmur. There were three cans in the path every Sunday morning. Everyone knew who left them. Everyone looked studiously at the ceiling.

"We want safety, too," Sharma said from the corner, arms folded. She'd come in uniform but poured coffee and took notes like a neighbor. "And hatch success. Those two things are not enemies if we think before we install."

"And if people aren't driving ATVs on the beach after midnight," Mark added, because momentum was a muscle and he was tired of letting it atrophy. "That's not just unsafe, it's illegal. The tracks are everywhere."

"Boys will be boys," someone muttered.

"Boys can be better," Sophie said, and the room quieted because she was the kind of kid adults listened to after they remembered themselves. "We were here last night with Paws. We saw lights and heard engines on the beach. If there's a baby turtle under the sand, it can't wear earplugs."

A few of the teenagers stared at their shoes in a way that wasn't quite guilt and wasn't quite defiance. One of them—tall, hair bleached by intent and not sun—raised his hand halfway. "We ride outside the ropes," he said. "Mostly."

"Mostly kills nests," Sharma said, and she didn't sugar it. "Look. This isn't punishment. It's stewardship. The ordinance keeps red light on the beach. The watch group does a couple of extra patrols during peak hatch. The rest is neighbor to neighbor. If you see tracks, take a photo. If you see someone ignoring the stakes, call it in or call me. None of this works unless we actually do it."

Polo Shirt scowled, then softened when he realized there were muffins. "Fine," he said. "We'll try the red bulbs. But if my insurance—"

"—goes down because your guests stop tripping on glare," Mark finished, almost cheerful now. "You'll tell your colleagues. They'll copy you. You'll look like a visionary at the Chamber breakfast."

A small laugh rolled through the room. Nobody liked the Chamber breakfasts.

In the back, a fisherman named Pike leaned his chair onto two legs and watched without speaking. He had a logo on his baseball cap no one recognized and a new truck that didn't have sand in the bed yet. When the meeting broke for coffee and cookies, he didn't move to the snacks. He only watched Sarah whisper to Sharma, eyes bright, asking about reporting forms. He watched Paws, too—the way the dog threaded through the people to rest against Sophie's shin, a pale, attentive shadow. Pike was good at clocks. He filed away how long it took the dog to cross the room, how many steps between the back door and the dune path.

After, in the spill of evening, Mark and Sarah walked the length of their stretch. The argument had been civil enough to feel like progress and sharp enough to leave a burr under Mark's tongue. Paws padded, quiet and proud of having resisted stealing a muffin. The air had cooled the way it only does near water, and the smell was clean, all salt and green and dusk.

Until it wasn't.

The metallic tang threaded back under the brine—a thin ribbon, like plumber's tape pulled tight. Paws stopped dead, nose up, and issued that low, resonant sound they had learned to follow. Sophie reached automatically for the back of his collar. Leo went still because Sophie went still; it was their relay of calm.

"Wind's south," Sarah said, already turning her face into it. "Not drains. This is offshore."

The horizon was a lid of pewter, thick and smooth. No navigation lights blinked. The hum rose, dipped, rose again. A pinprick beam flashed once very near the waterline—too low and too tight for a mast. Then gone.

Mark lifted his phone and opened the compass app, because if you were going to tell someone later, you should know what you were saying. "Bearing one-eight-six," he murmured, angling the screen. "Narrow-beam flashlight near the bar."

"Add it to the log," Sarah said, and Sophie nodded. She would print it later and pin it to the **Weird**

Things board in the kitchen behind the shopping list and the permission slips.

They stayed until the hum shifted west and thinned to nothing. When it was fully gone, Paws' tail lifted from storm position. He shook once, a dog's hard reboot, and blew a breath that warmed the circle of Sophie's wrist.

"Can we go home now?" Leo yawned.

"Yes," Sarah said. "And pie."

"Mrs. Gable's blueberry?" Sophie asked.

"Of course."

They were halfway to the boardwalk when a set of ATV headlights slashed the dune grass two blocks up, sharp white cutting through the new red glow of a porch bulb someone had installed that afternoon. The engine brapped twice—the adolescent peacock sound—and the machine made a tight, sandy loop entirely inside the roped-off swale.

Mark didn't think. He ran.

"Mark!" Sarah hissed, but he was already moving, anger quicker than breath. He didn't plan to catch them; he planned to be seen running and to be the kind of problem that made you slow down next time.

Paws bolted, then checked when Sophie's hand tightened. They watched from the shadow of a sea grape stand as the rider fishtailed and paused next to a second ATV at the lip of the path. Two teens—maybe three, it was hard to count heads in helmets. One lifted his visor and laughed the laugh that says *I don't live with consequences.* The other gestured toward the beach proper.

"Hey!" Mark shouted, voice ringing harder in the cool air than he'd meant. "Off the dune!"

The rider flinched, then revved, defiance as script. The second rider glanced toward the water—a reflex that betrayed him—and then both turned and tore up the path, sand spitting, engines loud in the quiet.

Mark stopped with his hands on his hips and his chest burning. He took a photo of the tracks with his phone. He took another of the line where the tires had cut the swale. He took a third of the face he made at the evening when he wanted it to do what he wanted. Then he walked back to his family, the adrenaline already curdling into embarrassment.

"Next time we call Sharma first," Sarah said, not unkind. "Then we yell."

"I hate this part," Mark said, air finally back in his lungs. "I hate knowing and watching and not having a badge."

"You have a dog," Sophie said, and Paws licked her knuckles like a point.

At home, they hung a dry-erase sheet by the back door because notes in a drawer were a type of forgetting. They wrote **LIGHTING**, **ATV**, **HUM**, **SHEEN** and left space under each to add dates and times. It looked like overkill. It looked like a plan.

Bills lived on the counter under a magnet shaped like a pelican. The insurance quote for hurricane coverage made Sarah sit down. Mark angled the paper under the lamp as if better light would soften the numbers. Paws put his chin on Sarah's knee, which worked better.

"It's fine," Mark said, because someone had to say it first. "We'll juggle. I'll take those two short contracts even if they're miserable. We can live leaner for a bit."

"I know how to live lean," Sarah said. "I just don't like knowing how far we can stretch before it snaps."

Sophie stood in the doorway and pretended she wasn't listening. She traced the seam where the paint met the hinge and told herself about sea stars instead. You could lose an arm and grow another if you had time and good water. Paws looked from one parent to the other and then to her, checking the pack.

Later, when the house breathed slow, Mark went back out to the porch with the red-lensed flashlight Sharma had given them. He rotated the filter into place and clicked the beam on and off, testing the quiet of it. Down the beach, three other porches glowed dim and kind. People changed faster than policy. He tried to let that be enough for one night.

The hum came and went twice in the dark hours, less sound than the memory of sound. Paws woke each time, lifted his head, and didn't bark. He put his chin back on his paws, one eye open, and watched the door.

Saturday brought a farmers' market and a second meeting, this one at the community hall with folding chairs that bit your thighs and a whiteboard that ghosted old arguments under new ones. The agenda had grown: lighting ordinance (vote), ATV enforcement (proposal), citizen watch group (interest), and "other business," which carried the weight of three unspoken stories.

A line of local business owners sat together as if proximity could make a bloc. A surfer with a taped knee leaned on the back wall. The drone boys slouched in the middle like they were being punished, which was maybe the point. Silas sat in the last row, arms crossed, eyes half-closed, listening like a dock listens to a boat bumping it.

"Red lighting ordinance," the chair announced. "Ranger Sharma to explain in no more than three minutes."

Sharma did it in two and a half with a poster and three sentences. "White light draws hatchlings inland. Red light does not. The difference is lives."

"Motion?" the chair asked.

"So moved," Mrs. Gable said, and there was a chorus of seconds.

"We'll need time to retrofit," Polo Shirt said, less combative now that he'd seen the muffins were free again. "But... fine."

"ATVs?" the chair said.

"Ban them," someone offered.

"They're already banned," Sharma said dryly, tapping the law printed at the bottom of the agenda. "We need enforcement and we need community memory.

37

Cameras at the three dune crossings. Signs at ankle height *and* eye level. If you ride, you're fined. If you ride twice, you lose your machine for the season."

A murmur. Someone asked who would pay for cameras. Someone else said fundraisers. Mark raised his hand. "I'll match the first five hundred dollars in donations," he said before he could think better of it. Sarah glanced sideways at him, then nodded once, as if she'd already moved three numbers in their budget to make it true.

"Citizen watch?" the chair said.

"Not vigilantes," Sharma cut in before anyone could get excited. "Observers. We walk. We log. We report. We don't confront unless safety requires it. We do it together so no one feels like a crank at one in the morning. We text each other when we see something. We agree not to post videos of teenagers being idiots; we send them to me instead. We hold each other accountable. That's the whole ballgame."

Hands went up. People signed a sheet. Sophie did, too, printing her name slowly and then adding **(with Paws)** in careful letters. No one crossed it out.

Under Other Business, a woman from the marsh edge raised a quiet hand. "The hum," she said. "Anyone else hearing it?"

Three more hands, then five. Silas' eyes opened all the way. "South bar," he said. "Between the two buoys. Not every night."

"It's legal to run dark if your lights are malfunctioning," a man said from the back in the tone of a person who likes exceptions. "Maybe they're just out of compliance."

"Maybe," Sharma said. "Or maybe it's something else. I'll flag it with the Coast Guard. In the meantime, keep logging. Bearings if you can. Don't go out there trying to play hero."

Paws lifted his head at the word *hero,* and Sophie hid a smile in his fur.

When the meeting broke, Pike slipped out the side door. Outside, on the shaded walk, he pulled his phone and typed a short message with one hand: **new dog, new eyes. watch the girl.** Then he pocketed the phone and walked toward a truck whose tires hadn't learned the sound of sand yet.

They built the habit of walking at dusk with intention. Not patrol—patrol sounded like wearing uniforms and adopting a posture—but presence. Presence that collected things: wrappers, bottle caps, the slender twist of fishing line that could strangle a gull's leg. Presence that nodded at neighbors and learned which porch lights had gone red. Presence that stopped when Paws stopped.

He stopped more often.

Sometimes it was for a treasure Leo would declare a dinosaur tooth (it wasn't). Sometimes it was for a cracked pail that might cut a foot. Sometimes it was for nothing they could see until Sophie crouched and found a newly scuffed patch where a stake had been, and a faint, sharp heel print not made by a child.

On the seventh night, at the edge of Heron's Cove, he put his nose to the seam between wet and dry sand and followed it like a stitched line. He didn't do the soft sound. He didn't stiffen. He simply traced. Sarah followed the same path with a red light held low and found a glint of something round, flat, and stamped with a logo she didn't recognize. Not a coin. A cap. Industrial.

She slid it into a bag without touching it and wrote the date, time, and tide on the outside. She put a star next to it.

By then, Mark had read the entire municipal code on public access and a white paper on hatch disorientation and was two-thirds through a Coast Guard field guide to small-boat navigation. It made him feel better to know what words meant. It made him feel worse to realize how many of the good ones—*jurisdiction, authority, resources*—belonged to other people.

They took their notes to Sharma. She took them seriously. She didn't promise them endings; she promised to listen and to show up. It was enough for now because the beginning of a story is the part where you decide whether your character will step outside when they hear a noise. They had stepped. They didn't plan to step back.

The night before the first storm of the season, the hum grew teeth. It wasn't louder; it was closer. Paws' body went from easy to *on* in a breath. His ears pricked and his weight shifted forward until the leash caught. Sophie tightened her grip without looking down.

"Mark," Sarah said, and he was already lifting the binoculars. Nothing on the horizon—a strip of lightless dark that swallowed shapes. Then: a low silhouette, too flat to be a sailboat, too fast to be a barge, moving with a confidence that made Mark's molars grind.

"Call it in," he said. "Now."

Sharma answered on the second ring. "Where?"

"Heron's Cove, outside the bar. No lights."

"On it," she said. "I'm two minutes from the station. Keep off the wet sand; we've had sloughs open up."

The boat angled, slowed, then idled in a patient, infuriating way. The wind shifted. The metallic tang crawled up the beach and slid into their mouths like a bad taste. Paws' low sound deepened. He leaned. Sophie whispered **stay** in the breath way and felt the answer ripple through his muscles.

Far out, a second hum threaded the first. Not echo. Response. For the first time since they'd arrived, Mark felt the shape of the thing they'd been circling: not a mistake, not *away,* but deliberate. He reached for Sarah's hand and found it already reaching for his.

"Dad," Sophie whispered. "They're here."

"Not for long," Sarah said, and her voice was the steel under everything gentle.

The storm broke the next day, flattening the beach and blowing the scent into the marsh where it hid in reeds and memory. When the rain cleared, there would be new lines in the sand, new edges, new places to look. There would be meetings and more notes and a dog whose low sound would become their metronome. There would be neighbors who turned porch lights red and others who didn't. There would be nights when the hum didn't come and nights when it did. There would be people who liked them and people who crossed the street.

There would be a story, and they were in it now, whether they'd planned to be or not.

On the porch that evening, as the first heavy drops hammered the steps, Sophie leaned into Paws' shoulder and felt the steady rise and fall that meant *here*. She pressed her face into his fur and let the storm wash the day clean.

"We're going to be okay," she told him.

He didn't know those words. He knew tone. He knew pack. He knew the smell of a thing that didn't belong and the way his girl's pulse slowed when he rested his head on her knee. He knew the difference between quiet and silence. He knew that when the door opened and the wind came in smelling of iron, his people got closer to one another.

He put his paw over Sophie's foot and kept it there until the rain softened and the hum, wherever it lived, lost interest for the night.

Chapter 3
THE MYSTERY DEEPENS

The storm cleaned the beach the way a stern teacher wipes a chalkboard—hard, fast, and without apology. By morning, the shoreline had shifted inches. The dune face wore a fresh bite; the wrack line had jumped, then braided itself into a new seam of eelgrass, kelp, and things the ocean had decided no longer belonged to it.

Paws trotted the margin like a surveyor. The air had that rinsed clarity storms leave behind, the sky a lean blue that made everything honest. He sniffed a battered length of rope, a clump of kelp beaded with sand fleas, a pale dome of horseshoe crab shell that looked like a helmet from a story Leo would love. Then his nose found something else—something that turned his posture from curious to intent.

"Wait," Sophie whispered, already matching his crouch. She'd learned to move the way he moved: quiet feet, low light, careful hands.

The "something else" looked unremarkable, which was why it mattered. Tiny translucent pellets studded the sand among the shells—smaller than peas, rounder than the beach's usual grit. They clicked when you pinched them; they didn't crush.

"Nurdles," Sarah said, because the word had lodged in her head years ago and came back now with the sour pride of recognizing a bad thing. She dug a sample bottle from her pack and held it out. "Polyethylene pre-production pellets. They float. They travel. They end up everywhere."

Sophie poured a little mound from her palm. "They look like fish eggs," she said, disgust and worried wonder mingling in her voice.

"They're meant to," Sarah said softly, more to herself. "Not in design, but in effect."

Mark scanned the wrack line the way he'd learned to scan spreadsheets: pattern first, then anomaly. The pellets trended thicker near the south end of the cove, thinner toward the point—no neat band, just a lean that suggested a source line offshore. He shaded his eyes. The bar was there as always, lurking barely underwater, its run a pale knuckle under the darker water. No boat, no light, no hum—not now. But the aftertaste of it remained.

"We log it." Sarah snapped the bottle cap with a practiced turn—one good habit cannibalized into another. "Tide, wind, location. We'll add it to the sheen, to the hum. We'll give Ranger Sharma something to put in her report."

Paws leaned into Sophie's knee and looked south. The storm had shoved a jag of driftwood high up the beach, the thick kind with scars that looked like writing. Nestled in its shadow was a smaller stash of human things the tide had not been able to drag away: a tangle of monofilament, a bent aluminum tag with three numbers stamped on it, a cheap flashlight scoured to foggy plastic.

"Gear dump?" Mark wondered, picking up the tag with two fingers and turning it so the light caught the stamp: **184**. "Or a catch-all from everywhere."

"Don't touch the lens," Sarah warned, even as he'd already not touched it. "Bag first, questions later."

They were becoming that family—the one with gloves in the beach bag and empty Ziplocs where sandwiches should have been. Sophie didn't mind. The bags were trophies when they were full.

By afternoon the wind had climbed again, and a warning line of clouds stacked over the horizon like a slow parade. The bakery was crowded with people making storm-adjacent purchases—bread that kept, muffins that felt like a good idea when the power inevitably blinked. Mrs. Gable slid a pie onto the counter and a note into Sarah's palm: *Town Hall 7 PM. Lighting vote. ATVs on the agenda. Bring that dog's halo if you've got one.*

"He doesn't need a halo," Sophie said, affronted on principle.

"He can borrow mine," Mrs. Gable winked. "Bless us, we're going to need all the angles."

Town Hall had seen better paint and worse meetings. Folding chairs sat in a grid that made people behave, and a whiteboard leaned against the front wall with

AGENDA written at a slant. The room smelled faintly of dust and lemon cleaner. A fan chopped the air without coolness.

The first part went easily: a unanimous vote for red-spectrum bulbs on all beachfront properties during hatch season, effective immediately. The harder part made the fan seem louder.

"We aren't out to ban fun," said a retiree with a sun-spotted forearm who'd spent thirty minutes that morning pulling tire tracks out of a nest site with a rake. "We're out to keep four tires off a beach that can't grow more sand."

A man in a fitted polo with a shoreline-real-estate logo on the chest raised his hand. "I rent to families who vacation on the beach precisely because they can *use* it. We're not talking about motorized marauders. We're talking about reasonable enjoyment."

"Reasonable doesn't include engines after dark," Sarah said, calm as flint. "And reasonable didn't include the tracks that crossed two posted wrack lines

51

last week. It didn't include the beers left in the dune path either, but here we are."

"The sheriff's office is handling the citations," the chair said, trying to be both firm and soothing and achieving neither. "What we need is buy-in."

"What you need is cameras at the three crossings," someone called from the back. "High, low, and hidden."

"It's a beach, not a prison," the real estate man protested.

"It's a nursery," Mrs. Gable countered, voice honeyed and unshakable. "Try whispering."

Ranger Anya Sharma stood when the murmurs threatened to turn into crisscrossed arguments. "Here's what I can offer," she said. "My crew will add two night patrols a week for the next six weeks. I can't promise more; the state cut our overtime in August. But I can offer training for a citizen watch—what to log, what to photograph, what not to do. You'll carry an ID card that says *Observer*. You won't approach unless someone is actively damaging a nest or placing a life in immediate danger. You will not post pictures of people being dumb on social media; you will text them to me. If you can commit to that, put your name on the sheet in the back."

She clicked a slide she didn't need—the image of a hatchling tangled in a twist of fishing line—and the room sighed as one organism.

"I'll help," Sophie said, already up, already writing her name. She added **(with Paws)** and drew the tiniest paw print because she could not help herself.

From the doorway, a man in a ball cap watched the small motion of her pen. Pike had the patience of a fisherman and the eye of someone who counted exits. He held the door too long when he left, then let it close silently.

The first hatch of the week came three nights later—no storm, just heat coming off the sand like breath and stars caged by a thin haze. Sarah felt the telltale crumble in the nest's crust with the ball of her foot and stopped so suddenly Sophie walked into her. Paws froze because she did.

"Capping," Sarah whispered. "Listen."

There it was: the faintest papery rustle under the sand. A single grain slid, then another. The nest was a shallow dome with a depression centered like a thumbprint. At the rope, a new sign swung: **IF YOU SEE HATCHLINGS: RED LIGHTS ONLY. KEEP PATHS DARK. CALL RANGER SHARMA.**

"On it," Mark said, phone already in hand. "Sharma's five minutes out."

They killed their lamps and let their eyes chew the dark. After an eternity that was ten minutes, the first hatchling broke the surface like a magic trick: a coin-sized head, two blunt flippers startling the air. It pushed, sand avalanched, and another head surfaced, then another. The nest vibrated with life.

"Hello, little ancestors," Sarah breathed.

Then a light flared white farther down the beach.

"Hey!" someone called cheerfully, oblivious to their own brightness. "Look, kids—baby turtles!"

"Red light!" Mark called back, trying for friendly and landing on urgent. "Please—red filters only!"

Two adults shielded their flashlight with their palms in a way that made no difference. The hatchlings closest to the glow pivoted inland, tiny faces set toward the wrong stars.

"Paws," Sophie whispered, and the dog—trained, brilliant, wholly himself—stepped sideways and planted his body like a low wall. He didn't bark. He didn't need to. His shadow cut the spill of light, turning it from a blazing lure into a muted halo. The hatchlings corrected, flippers sweeping little commas across the sand.

The white light dipped; the red lens clicked into place. "Sorry!" the man called, chastened. "Sorry, sorry!"

Ranger Sharma jogged up moments later, breathing hard. She grinned once at the nest, then set to work in that clean, efficient way she had. "Guard right there," she told Paws, as if the dog were officially on her team. He blinked solemnly and stayed exactly where he was, tail pressed flat, head low.

They shepherded the clutch with patience: Sarah loosening crust for the slow ones, Mark sweeping the path clear of pebbles, Sophie counting in a whisper and carrying the two who veered inland despite everything. Ninety-three made it to the runout, then into the black water—tiny strokes, tiny shadows absorbed into the larger dark.

"Good odds," Sharma said when the sand settled and the night breathed again. "As good as I've seen this summer."

"Because of you," the white-light man said to Paws, with the zeal of a new convert. "Oh, you're a genius. You're... a saint."

"He'll take pie," Mrs. Gable said from behind them, materializing with a thermos like she routinely appeared at miracles. "Saint Paws prefers blueberry."

They laughed because they needed to. Then the wind turned, bringing a faint, metallic tang that wiped the smile off Mark's mouth.

Sharma felt it, too. She tipped her head to the south, eyes narrowing. "Hear that?"

The hum wasn't loud. It was a suggestion more than a sound. But they knew it now—tone, tempo, the way it sawed across the air like a bad idea. The ocean beyond the bar held a shape darker than dark, moving without running lights, self-assured as a thief in his own house.

Sharma's hand went to her radio. "Station, this is Ranger Sharma at marker E-7. Possible unlit vessel south of Heron's Cove, bearing..." She glanced at Mark, who had already lifted his phone. "One-eight-five. Requesting Coast Guard visibility ping."

Static, then a voice. "Copy, E-7. Cutter Polaris ten minutes out of channel. Station drone launching."

"Don't," Sharma said under her breath. "Not the drone, not tonight."

But the drone was already up—a wasp-whine to match the boat's hum. It banked south, its eye a tiny fevered glow. It drew a line out to the sulking shape beyond the bar and hovered there, all curiosity and no weight.

"Kids," Sharma said. "Back to the path."

The boat out past the bar altered course so minutely you could miss it if you didn't know you were watching. Then a pencil of light cut the drone from below—a vicious, perfect spear. The drone blinked, faltered, and dropped. It hit the water with a sound that was not much sound at all, then sunk without ceremony.

"Laser," Mark said, throat dry.

"Or aim," Sharma said. She didn't swear. It would have been the right place for it. "Polaris, be advised target is equipped to counter drone surveillance. Requesting caution."

"Copy," the radio said tightly. "We'll keep our mirrors on. ETA eight."

The dark shape held position like a dare. Then it slid west, out of the line where anyone shore-based could track it. The hum thinned, then disappeared behind the static of the larger sea.

"Okay," Sharma said to no one and everyone. "That's new. And bad."

Paws let out that low, held note—the one they had come to think of as the metronome of their summer. Sophie's fingers found his collar without looking.

"Home," Sarah murmured. "Now."

They walked fast without running. The sand seemed to want to hold their ankles. At the boardwalk, someone had hung a new sign under the lighting ordinance notice. The paper was thick, the ink a crude block script.

KEEP YOUR DOG OUT OF OTHER PEOPLE'S BUSINESS.

There was no signature. There never is.

Mark took a photo. Sarah took the paper down and folded it once, precisely, before sliding it into her bag.

"Do we—" Sophie began.

"We tell Sharma," Sarah said. Her voice was steady enough to make the rest of them steady, too. "And we buy brighter red bulbs. And we don't stop."

Paws pressed against Sophie's hip all the way home. In the kitchen they hung the note on the **Weird Things** board right next to the baggie with the aluminum tag stamped 184 and the photo of the drone boys' lost wasp. Sophie drew a small, unadorned paw print next to the words **other people's business** and then an arrow to **our beach.**

Morning pressed everything back into ordinary shapes, because that's what morning does. Leo built a city of sand beside the porch steps; Paws supervised with the serious face he wore for all civil engineering. Mark tried to work in the attic and succeeded for forty-seven minutes. Sarah paid the power bill, then reorganized the drawer where the good scissors go to die.

At ten, a white SUV rolled into the drive. It didn't have a light bar; it had a departmental seal stuck on with what looked like honest pride. A man in a county polo got out holding a tablet and a smile that might have been real, and might have been defense.

"Ben Carter," he said, offering the tablet like a handshake. "County Environmental Enforcement. Ranger Sharma asked me to look at your log."

"Lieutenant Carter," Sarah said, because she read name tags like other people did crosswords. "Come in."

He read the entries standing at their counter—dates, times, bearings, tiny notes in Sarah's neat hand: **smell metallic**; **man in cap at meeting**; **ATV at dune cut, two riders, one visor up—possible Brandon Pike?** His mouth tightened once. He flicked back to the photo of the sign from the boardwalk and shook his head.

"Classic," he said. "Anonymity is a hell of a drug."

"You think it's connected?" Mark asked. "The hum, the pellets, the drone, the note?"

"I think it's a small town," Carter said. "Everything's connected."

He set the tablet down and scratched Paws between the ears like they'd agreed on that before. "Listen. If you want out, say the word. We can take it from here."

Sophie's look could have sanded paint. "We're not getting out."

Carter smiled with the quick surprise of someone who remembers being eleven and certain. "Good. Then let me do something for you. I can't deputize a dog. But I can fit him with a reflective harness and a badge that says *observer*. It won't mean anything in court. It will make people think twice."

"Paws will love a vest," Sophie breathed, as if this were the pinnacle of canine ambition.

"And," Carter added, slanting a glance at Mark, "I can make sure your porch camera is admissible if it ever needs to be. Move it six inches left. Lose the novelty sign. The judge we have now has a sense of humor only in even years."

They moved the camera.

They lost the novelty sign (a rusted mermaid who used to say **NO SHOES, NO SHIRT, NO PROBLEM**).

Paws accepted the harness with gravitas and then, because he was Paws, tried to lick Carter's nose. Carter laughed, a sound that loosened something that had been tight since the drone went under.

"Look," he said at the door. "There are a lot of ways this goes. Some of them are boring. Some of them are not. If it turns into *not,* you don't get points for being first to the front. You call us. You let the people with radios be brave."

"We're not brave," Sarah said. "We're stubborn."

"Even worse," Carter said, pleased. "Stubborn people change things."

That night, the tide went out farther than it had in a week. The bar showed its knuckles, and the channel at Serpent's Tongue darkened to a blue so dense it was almost black. Silas stood on the point with a cigarette he didn't light and counted the beats between waves like you measure a pulse.

"Bad water for strangers," he said as the Reynolds came up the path. "Good water for knowing what you're doing. Tell your dog thanks for the turtles."

"He's reading your mind," Sophie said, because Paws was watching Silas as if he'd spoken in whisker-language. The old man's mouth turned up—not a smile, exactly, but the nearest weather to one.

"You keep your eyes on the Tongue," he said quietly to Mark. "People who cut it at night because they think they're clever, they leave pieces of themselves. If you see any of those pieces washed up that look like more than they should be, you tell Carter. Don't touch. Not even with a stick."

"We found an aluminum tag," Mark said. "Stamped numbers. One-eight-four."

"Could mean anything," Silas said, which is what you say when it could mean many things and none of them are good. "Could mean nothing. Could be a bait box. Could be a list. Don't put it in your pocket."

Paws sniffed the wind, then leaned against Sophie's calf. Far out, the hum started—thin, then fuller, then thinning again, like a singer warming up a throat. They watched until the light failed and the first stars shouldered their way into view.

"You tell your dog he's doing the Lord's work," Silas said as he turned to go.

"He's Jewish," Sarah said automatically, then smiled because surprises like that were a small, necessary joy.

"Even better," Silas said. "They keep better notes."

They stood together in the kind dark, their shoulders a small, sturdy line against the ocean's larger one. The waves spoke in their old idiom—advance, retreat, polish, erase—and the hum threaded through like a new accent you didn't want to learn but were going to anyway.

On the walk home, Sophie touched the badge on Paws' harness and felt the tiny give of the stitched edge. It wasn't armor. It wasn't proof. It was a promise: to watch, to write it down, to keep walking. Above them, porch after porch burned red. It looked, for a moment, like a constellation had fallen to earth and tried to teach them something about being points in a pattern: separate, necessary, bright enough to guide.

Chapter 4
THE TONGUE'S EDGE

B y late morning the gym at the community center smelled like coffee and old varnish. Ranger Anya Sharma stood at half-court with a flip chart and the face of someone who'd slept three hours and chosen a crisp uniform over regret. A cardboard box of red headlamp filters sat beside her sneakers. Ben Carter leaned on the stage with a tablet and a rolled posterboard he'd already threatened to turn into a legal lecture.

"Citizen Watch isn't cosplay," Sharma began. "You're observers. You record. You don't escalate. If you see an immediate threat to a person or protected wildlife, you call nine-one-one and me. Otherwise, your job is to be boring." She smiled just enough to keep the room with her. "Boring builds cases."

Paws lay sphinxed at Sophie's feet in his new reflective harness, the little *OBSERVER* badge stitched crooked on purpose because that was how Sophie had wanted it. He blinked at the room like he'd been appointed to the bench.

Carter took over. "Three rules," he said, unscrolling the poster with a neatly printed list. "One: photographs beat anecdotes. Two: time stamps and landmarks beat 'I think it was around there.' Three: people get mad; we stay polite." He flicked to a slide on his tablet—an aerial of the coastline with dots at crossings, nest sites, and the cut called Serpent's Tongue. "We'll assign zones. You'll pair up. Night patrols get radios. Yes, we know you can text; no, we don't trust it when it matters."

He handed out laminated cards with helpline numbers and the words **SUNSET BEACH OBSERVER** at the top. Paws got a pat from a retired nurse. A teenager in a surf shop hoodie asked if "observer" meant he could tell tourists to stop chasing ghost crabs. "You can tell them please," Carter said. "You can't tell them or else."

Sharma fitted filters over headlamps, clipped spare batteries to lanyards, and demonstrated the low sweep of a red beam over sand—the way you lit a path without turning it into a runway. "Our predators cue on brightness," she said, meaning gulls and meaning men. "Keep it dim and keep it steady."

Two hours later the gym emptied with the hush of people who were leaving with more responsibility than they'd arrived with. Mrs. Gable pressed a muffin into Sophie's hand. "Fuel," she said. "For saints and dogs."

At the hardware store, the new rack of red bulbs had a hand-lettered sign: **FOR TURTLES. ALSO FOR MOOD.** Mark grabbed four and a spool of biodegradable twine. He was halfway to the counter when a man's laugh, just a shade too loud, snagged him.

"Hey, hero." Brandon Pike—cap backward, jaw set like a man who'd never met a rule he didn't resent—leaned on a stack of coolers. "How's your watchdog? Hear he got himself a badge."

"He got a vest," Mark said, evenly. "The badge is for the people."

"Cute," Pike said. "Maybe teach him to read trespass signs."

Mark paid, felt the old itch to explain himself, didn't scratch it. On the way out he almost plowed into a woman in a blazer holding a glossy tri-fold. **DORAN COASTAL DESIGN** curved over a photo of a boardwalk at sunset.

"You're Mark Reynolds," she said like they had an appointment. "I'm Lila from Doran. We're revitalizing the south-end promenade. Heard you do project management with an engineering background."

"What kind of revitalizing?" Mark asked, because it was easier than saying he was currently doing spreadsheets at his kitchen table.

"Wider walk, new kiosks, lighting that says 'open for business.' We want community input." She tapped the brochure. "And a local lead who can keep contractors on schedule. Good pay. Quick timeline."

"What kind of lighting?"

She smiled the way people do when they think you didn't hear the word "pay." "Safe lighting. Bright. Family-friendly."

"Red-spectrum at the beach face and shielded," Mark said. "No uplight. No spill."

She tilted her head. "We're working within code."

"Code's the floor," he said, surprised at how quickly the sentence showed up. "If you want the job done right, it's red and shielded. If you want it done fast, it's not me."

She held his gaze for a beat longer than polite. "If you change your mind," she said lightly, pressing a card into his palm. "Schedules have a way of getting real."

He tucked the card in his pocket like a rock you meant to throw back later and didn't.

The afternoon tide fell away in long exhalations, leaving behind tide pools rimmed with periwinkles and a skim of rainbow slick that looked pretty if you didn't know better. Sarah crouched by a pool no bigger than a hubcap. The iridescence shivered when she tapped it—breaks and re-forms: true sheen, not plankton.

"Same smell," she murmured. Sweet-metallic, like pennies and solvent. She drew a sample with a glass pipette, snapped the vial, labeled it **E-7 Pool/1530** in neat block letters. Paws made a face and sneezed twice, offended.

"Can you track it?" Sophie asked him, because she always asked and because sometimes he could.

He put his nose to the ripple of water draining seaward and then to the trickle that led landward, into the thatch of crushed Spartina at the toe of the dune. He looked back at Sarah, then into the grass, then back, the way you look at someone when you've already told them the answer three times.

"All right," Sarah said. They moved inland, careful feet on tough grass. The thin trickle widened to a palm's width where someone had pressed a channel with something heavy. At the edge of the dune a clump of beach heather looked a little too perfect. Paws stood rigid, tail low.

"What do you smell?" Sophie asked, her hand on his shoulder. He exhaled hard, almost a huff, then pawed once at the sand and stopped, the way he did when his instinct to dig ran headfirst into training.

Mark brushed aside the heather with a gloved hand. Blue paint winked up from the sand—barrel-blue, industrial. A drum lay half-buried in a hollow, its lid scorched around the bung hole, a chain embossed in the sand where someone had dragged it, then tried to cover the trail with their feet.

Sarah's mouth went dry. "Don't touch it." She stepped back, the way you step back from a snake you didn't know was there. "Ben first. Then Anya."

Carter answered on the second ring. "I'm six minutes out," he said, and somehow made that sound like both comfort and warning. "Back ten feet. No... back twenty. Wind at your back? Good. Don't light anything. Don't be heroes."

"Birds," Sophie whispered, looking at a pair of plovers three yards away, their nervous little feet stitching the sand. "We can't just—"

"We step back," Sarah said, gently but absolute. "We do it right."

The six minutes took twelve. In the ninth minute, a stone clipped the heather overhead and fell into the sand with a thud that felt louder than it was. Paws went from rigid to coiled. He didn't bark. He looked toward the line of sea grape and oak where the shade thickened.

Mark turned slow, chin up, eyes down. "Don't," he said quietly to the dark. "You already forgot something."

Another stone fell, closer, theatrical. Sophie's fingers dug into the harness strap at Paws' shoulder. He quivered but held. Training and trust and a child's hand—sometimes that's all that stands between a dog doing what he wants and doing what he's learned.

Carter came in from the access path at a fast walk, two county guys behind him with a hard-sided case and faces that said they'd rather be anywhere else. He took one look at the barrel and didn't come closer than fifteen feet.

"Photographs," he said without looking away from the drum. "Perimeter. Then we all go hydrate somewhere far away while I make a lot of phone calls."

The county guys laid a painted stake near the dragged channel and another at the heather. Carter shot the drum with the long lens on his tablet, frowning at the scorch. "Somebody tried to burn off residue," he said. "Somebody who knows just enough to be dangerous."

He finally looked up. "Anyone throw rocks at you?"

"Rocks threw themselves," Mark said.

"Classic," Carter repeated, like he had an ongoing private conversation with the word.

They backed away the way they'd come. Paws moved on Sophie's exhale. When they reached the boardwalk, Carter rested a hand on the dog's harness—one quick, grateful press. "Good hold," he said. Paws accepted the praise like a paycheck.

Behind them, the county guys unrolled bright tape and threaded it through the stakes. The drum sat there like an accusation.

"You sure you want me seeing this?" Silas asked that night on the porch, the drum tape still in his head the way some songs get. "A man sleeps better when he can say he doesn't know."

"You already don't sleep," Sarah said, and slid the photo across the table. The scorch on the lid had the ugly symmetry of something done twice.

Silas grunted. "Torch job," he said. "Fast hands, dumb outcome."

"You seen that stamp?" Mark asked, pushing over a second photo—the tag they'd found by the drift pile, **184** punched into cheap aluminum. "We keep tripping over this number."

"Could be a bait box," Silas said. "Could be a list. Could be fifty other things." He reached in his jacket and pulled out a folded chart so old the creases had creases. Pencil lines ran down the margin where the bar was marked in soundings, shallow water annotated with a crabbed hand. One corner showed the Serpent's Tongue, arcing like a question mark.

"My father marked slacks," he said, tapping his finger on a penciled X. "Where you could cut without God and the Coast Guard noticing. That was before everybody put lights on their toys and called it progress. You want to watch men who think they're clever? Watch here." He tapped again. "Half hour on either side of the Tuesday low. Less chop. Less witness."

Ben Carter's card sat under the salt shaker. Sarah slid the chart's corner under it like an anchor. "We'll tell him," she said.

"You'll tell him," Silas agreed. "And then you'll pretend you don't know how to sit in a car with the lights off. Let the paid ones be brave."

Sophie had Paws' head in her lap and was tracing his ear with one finger the way she did when she was thinking. "We could just... watch," she said. "From the turnout. With the red lights off."

Silas grunted again, which they'd learned translated to *you will, because you are you.*

They didn't call it a stakeout. They called it *watching the stars from the turnout that happened to face the Tongue* and didn't forgive themselves for the semantics.

The turnout sat high, west of the access road, where the low scrub gave way to an abrupt edge and an unkind view of the dark water threading between shoals. They rolled in at nine, lights off, engine cut. The air had that damp sea-coolness that made you feel like you could breathe more and think less. The truck's dash clock glowed a private time. Paws put his

80

chin on the window sill and fogged the glass with a soft question.

"Think of it like camping," Mark said, and nobody believed him.

At nine twenty a pickup eased down the access road with its headlights off and its parking lights on, the way people do when they know that what they're doing looks worse in full illumination. It stopped by the last trash barrel before the sand. The driver didn't get out. The passenger did, fast and tight. He carried something that looked like a duffel and moved like he'd practiced.

Mark lifted the camera, careful to shield the screen. The shutter sound was a mechanical cough he'd never noticed until now. The passenger cut left of the barrel and into the grass where the footpath widened, approached the shadow where that afternoon's drum had been, and stopped short as if surprised to find tape. He hesitated, then veered farther south, toward the deeper dark.

"Plate," Sarah breathed.

The pickup wore a plate, and the plate wore a chrome fish cutout half-covering two numbers. Mark zoomed, steadied, shot, shot again. The passenger reappeared without the bag, hopped in, and the truck rolled out slow.

"Partial," Mark said, lowering the camera, heart weird in his throat. "Eight-three and the fish eats the rest."

"Send it," Sarah said, already texting the photos to Carter without the part of her brain that likes to explain. **Turnout. 21:27. South access. Plate partial 83 with fish vanity. Two men. One bag.**

Carter's reply came back fast. **Stay put. Polaris on outside. County unit rolling your way. Do not follow.**

They didn't follow. They listened to the truck's tires chew shell and then the quiet return. Paws didn't whine. He watched the space the pickup had been like it might come back if he held its outline long enough.

The county unit turned up five minutes later, lights off, the entire posture of it apologetic and alert. Carter texted again: **Good pull. Go home.**

They did. The house looked softer than it had any right to; the red bulbs on the porch eased the shape of it into the night. On the top step lay a fish wrapped in nylon net, its silver eye dried to a marble. A rectangle of cardboard sat on its belly. **STAY IN YOUR LANE** in block letters. Below it, a big looping smiley face.

Paws' growl was low enough it felt like a bass note in the boards.

Mark picked up the cardboard with two fingers and slid it into a clean bag from the *Weird Things* drawer. Sarah lifted the fish by the trailing net and laid it gently in a bucket. "Anya first thing," she said. "And bleach for the step."

Sophie didn't say anything. She crouched, placed her hand on Paws' shoulders, and waited for his breathing to match hers. When it did, she stood, turned, and flicked the porch light off and on once like a lighthouse. It was a small, stubborn thing to do. It felt like exactly the right size.

The next morning the beach was loud with the ordinary—the scrape of rakes pulling lines smooth, the thwap of a volleyball, the shorebirds' cranky gossip. Leo announced the architecture of his sand city to a passing toddler with the gravity of a planning commissioner. Paws lay in the shade of the umbrella and accepted admiring remarks like a statesman.

Lila from Doran walked by in a crisp dress and bare feet that had never met a nail. She paused. "We could use someone like you," she said without preamble.

"Someone like me won't build you floodlights," Mark said without looking up from the list he was making: **bulbs, tape, sample vials, batteries, dog treats**.

She laughed, not unkind. "You'll call me when your schedule gets real."

He almost said *my schedule is real*. Instead he said, "We'll be at the council meeting Thursday. Bring your dark-sky spec."

She lifted a shoulder. "We work within code."

"Code's the floor," he repeated, and now it felt less like defiance and more like remembering your own spine.

When she left, Sarah said, "You could take the job and still do it right."

"I could," Mark said. "Or I could spend six months arguing over light shields and lose my mind."

"We already lost that," she said dryly, and they both laughed because it was that or grind their teeth.

In the afternoon, Cameron from the Coast Guard—everyone called him Cam because he insisted and because it was hard to hold his title and his youth in the same mouth—showed up with a knuckle of metal the size of a coin.

"Recovered it near the Tongue," he said, turning the metal so the light caught a stamped number. **184**. "Could be labeling for cut-lines on nets. Could be cargo tag. Polaris saw nothing that looked like a boat because the boat didn't want to be seen."

Sharma, who had arrived with Cam and a clipboard she'd beaten into submission, set the metal next to the photo of the drum lid. "You keep finding their breadcrumbs," she said. "They think that makes them clever. It makes them sloppy."

Carter, on speaker, said, "Sloppy gets tired. Tired gets caught."

"An anonymous note gets braver," Sarah said, and heard the way her voice thinned when it wanted to do the opposite.

"Which is why you keep your porch light red and your dog on a leash," Carter said. "And why I called the judge at breakfast. He hates me now. Congratulations, you're officially under the county's very small wing."

"Does that wing come with a force field?" Mark asked.

"It comes with more patrols at dumb hours," Carter said. "And a PO Box where people who are tired of Pike can mail me love letters."

"Pike," Sarah said.

"His name keeps coming up," Carter admitted. "Man's got a side hustle and a temper. But this is bigger than a hothead in a hat. Boats, barrels, lasers. This is a supply chain. We pull at all of it."

After they left, the house felt briefly, oddly empty—the way places do after officials depart, taking their certainty and their paperwork with them. Paws put his head on Sarah's knee and sighed a long, theatrical sigh.

"I know," she told him. "Witnessing is exhausting."

The next time the tide fell low enough to bare the bar, Silas showed up at the turnout with a thermos that could only have contained coffee strong enough to argue with. He sat on the hood like a man who'd sat on a thousand hoods and kept his eyes on the Tongue.

"They'll try again," he said without drama. "Because men like that don't know when to count their luck and go home."

The water slicked dark through the cut. Far offshore, something bigger than a skiff moved just enough to be a rumor. Paws lifted his head and watched the same spot like it had spoken.

"Ben's at the access," Sarah said. "Anya's at E-7. Cam's aboard Polaris. We're... watching the stars."

"You're telling yourself that," Silas said mildly. "You're also making sure the people who get paid to be brave aren't alone. There are worse sins."

Lights pricked on at the south access, then off—Carter's way of letting them know he was there without letting everyone else know. The night breathed. The ocean made its old, patient argument. Paws leaned an inch into Sophie's knees and held very still.

When the pickup finally turned down the access again, it didn't stop at the barrel tape. It drove straight into it, tore the bright ribbon free, and chewed up the path like it belonged. Carter's radio crackled. Headlights strobed from the dune line—white-white-red-blue, the county unit with its restraint gone. The pickup spun in a panicked K-turn, a fish plate flashing. "Eighty-three," Sophie breathed, fierce with triumph and fear. "Eight-three—"

"Got it," Carter's voice came thin from the radio. "Got it."

The truck clawed up the access road and, for a moment, filled the turnout with heat and light. The driver's face, young and self-convinced, flickered through the truck's window. The passenger's hat—flat brim, logo—flashed. Paws let out a sound that was not bark and not whine; it was a held note, exactly the pitch of a wire pulled tight.

Then the truck was gone, the county unit chasing. The light fell away. The night stitched itself closed as if it had never been cut.

Silas exhaled. "Bad water for strangers," he said again, softer. "Good water for men who know when to go slow."

They sat there until the stars reasserted themselves and the Tongue hummed with nothing but tide. When they climbed down, Paws hopped lightly to earth and shook out his coat as if shedding the weight of an hour.

"Tomorrow," Sarah said, very quietly, to the dark that had filled back in, "we plant more grass."

Mark squeezed her hand once. "And buy more vials."

"And keep our porch red," Sophie said, already counting steps down the path in rhythm with Paws' tail. "And teach people to whisper at the nursery."

"And tape your weird sign to the *Weird Things* board," Leo added from nowhere, appearing in pajama pants and a determined face. He held up a new cardboard rectangle, written in block letters of his own: **OUR LANE IS THE BEACH.**

Paws bumped it with his nose and the ink smudged just a little, proof that it was new and exactly theirs.

Chapter 5
The Bar Drawn Tight

By midafternoon the command post was a half-built thing of folding tables, duct tape, and intent. The county had parked a boxy mobile unit in the lot behind the bathhouse; the Coast Guard had draped a fiber line to a gray dome camera that pointed its unblinking glass eye toward the Serpent's Tongue. Somebody had zip-tied a laminated tide chart to a sawhorse.

A second sawhorse wore a hand-lettered sign: KIDS' CORNER — DRAW A TURTLE, SAVE A TURTLE. Mrs. Gable stood behind it dispensing crayons the way a pharmacist dispenses relief.

Paws worked a slow circuit along the perimeter tape, nose skimming the air, cataloging. Diesel, tar, the iron breath of wet tools. Under it, new threads: hot plastic, citrus solvent, a ghost of ozone. He paused at the tailgate of Anya's truck where a pelican case sat, closed with two padlocks and a strip of evidence tape, and took one long, thoughtful draw. He sneezed once—judgment passed, filed—and moved on.

Anya was all edges and economy. "Thirty-second brief," she said, voice carving the chatter clean. "You know your lanes. Dune observers behind tape. No white lights. If you have to use light, red filters only, beams down. You see a hatchling boil, you call in. You do not touch without verbal from a ranger. County is staged at north and south access; Coast Guard patrol offshore. The Tongue looks open at low, but it's cropping. I want you to assume anyone crossing it at speed is either lucky or reckless. Either way, we make them stop being both."

Carter stood with his thumbs hooked in his belt, face the color of an eraser. "Warrants in the wind," he said. "As soon as we have hands on a live act, we have paper to open sheds, boats, and a very ugly couch. Boring builds cases. Boring wins in front of a judge. Smash in your diary later."

Silas leaned against a post like he'd been born part driftwood. He tapped the paper chart where LOW TIDE 22:36 glowed in yellow highlighter. "They'll want the last twenty minutes going out," he said.

"Enough time to set their little piano keys on the bar and still walk boxes out without getting their jeans wet."

"Cam," Anya said toward the open radio on the table, "talk to me."

"Polaris stationed half a mile outside the Tongue," Cam's voice came tinny through the speaker—cheerfully tired, caffeine and salt welded together. "FLIR up. We've got a soft contact moving east of the jetty; looks like a skiff running dark, might be legit—guy with crab pots. I'll paint him if he turns dumb."

Mark checked the checklist on his clipboard as if it had some kind of power in it. Batteries topped, body cams time synchronized, spare red gels, vials for water sampling, sterile swabs, zip bags. He felt wired tight and weightless, like the night was a thing he'd strapped on and was going to have to wear until it stopped looking strange in the mirror.

Sophie stationed herself where she could see the dunes and the KIDS' CORNER both. Leo had a job so serious it shook him: pass out turtle stickers only to kids who could answer one question about the beach. He quizzed a six-year-old on dune grass with the gravity of a judge.

Paws came to heel on Sarah's left, leaned in until his shoulder touched her shin—calibration, confirmation. Sarah breathed through her nose and let the ritual settle her. "We do the boring," she told herself. "We keep the truth louder than the lie."

The day stretched itself into evening. Shadows lengthened. The heat loosened its grip. The ocean breathed like a big animal laying itself down.

At 20:47, the first decoy arrived: a pair of red chemical lights bobbing low along the waterline a quarter mile south, winking like drunk sirens. Two boys in high school hoodies lobbed them toward the surf, then melted into the sea oats. They would have been invisible without Cam's cold eye.

"Two juveniles flinging glow sticks," Cam reported. "Silly, not criminal. I'll keep an eye."

Anya didn't bother to look. "Let it be silly," she said. "Save my attention for clever."

It felt like a stage right before curtains. Even the gulls seemed to hold their throats.

And then, bang, the shift: not one big thing but five small ones in fast succession. The wind veered a point and began to smell of deep water. The generator hum—thin metal, off-key—returned from somewhere in the scrub, not where it had been last night. A white rectangle of work light popped alive north, where no one should have been able to drag a cord. The HUM became two HUMS. A third light banged alive farther south. A fourth—more distant—flickered over the Tongue itself like a promise.

"False lights," Sarah said into the radio. "Multiple. North dune face, south cut, and a free radical on the bar."

"Copy," Anya said, already moving. "All observers kill beams. Red filters only. Do not approach the fixtures. County, park at the gates, engines off. Cam, hold that bar light."

"Already holding," Cam said. "That's a lantern on a stick. Whoever set it had waders and a bad sense of humor."

The command post red-lit itself with a practiced twitch. The KIDS' CORNER became a cave of whispers. Mrs. Gable's hands moved children as if they were glass.

Paws froze. His whole body narrowed into purpose; his nose cut the air in lines. He turned his head toward the north dune as if it had spoken and then pointed—his tail stiff, his paw lifted, every cell of him saying *there*.

Sophie felt the message climb her bones. "Mom," she breathed. "He's got something."

Sarah crouched, one hand on the dog's ruff. His pulse thudded steady under her palm; the hum of the generator made a strange harmony with it. She looked where he looked and saw—nothing. But once you've learned to trust a dog that knows his own world, you stop insisting the world use your eyes.

"Observer One repositioning ten yards north," Sarah whispered into the radio. "Behind tape. Paws has a scent."

"Hold your line," Anya said. "We have rangers moving on the fixtures. Cam...?"

"Boat," Cam said, voice flattening with focus. "Two contacts at the Tongue, low and fast, coming from the west. No lights. Looks like they're trying to split the bar at the flat."

Carter's voice sharpened into steel. "County south, start rolling to the Tongue lot. North, stay put. We'll pinch them from both ends if they come ashore. Do not spook the deer before they hit the snare."

On the water, the dark shapes moved like bad ideas that had learned to swim. One angled toward the spit;

the other held farther out, riding the shallow like a dare. Their wakes made white scars in the slack water.

"Polaris moving," Cam said, and the radio picked up the distant change in the ocean when a cutter the size of a neighborhood starts to think about work. "I'll nose in enough to make a point."

At the north dune, Ranger Alvarez cut the power to the first work light clean. The white rectangle died; the night took a breath. "One down," he reported. "Cord runs into the sea grape. Whoever set it has long legs."

"Two down," Ranger Keahi said from the south cut. "Generator under a pallet. Extension cord boxed with sea oats. Whoever set it has the ethics of a raccoon."

"Leave the boxes," Anya said. "Photograph. Document. We'll collect once we have bodies."

Bodies—meaning suspects, not victims—but the word wore an edge anyway.

Paws' tail ticked once. He leaned forward, then checked himself when the leash tightened. *"Stay,"* Sarah whispered, and he did, quivering on *go*.

At the Tongue, the closer skiff swung on its prop and tried to come left, hugging the flat like a cat rubbing a chair. The farther one aimed straight at the lantern on the stick, as if stupid was the only strategy.

"Announcing," Cam said. The radio picked up the amplified hail—calm, patient, the voice of authority that has practiced saying please professionally: "Unlit vessel at the sandbar, this is the United States Coast Guard. Cut your engine. Repeat, cut your engine."

The nearer skiff pretended to hesitate. The farther one goosed the throttle and made a run. Its bow kissed the bar—and the bar bit back. The skiff lifted, lurched, and hung itself on its own momentum. A man stumbled, fell, got up swearing.

"Hooked," Cam said, satisfaction an inch under the word. "We're on approach."

The nearer skiff gunned away, trying to use the misfortune of its partner as distraction. It made fifteen yards of luck, then ten yards of arrogance, then found a shallow tooth of the bar and scraped its belly hard enough to cough smoke.

"County south, I'll take your right," Carter snapped. "Deputy Morales, you hold the access and stop anything with a bed and bad intentions."

"Copy," Morales said, breath already up. "My bed is made."

"Anya," Sarah said, low, "we've got movement north. Paws says there's a rabbit in the brush."

"Hold," Anya said. "I'm three dunes away."

And then the brush produced not a rabbit but a man—Pike—streaking along the back of the dune with the balance of someone who knew where the sand would hold and where it would roll. He dropped onto the access path like punctuation and sprinted toward the south lot. His cap was gone; his jaw had turned into someone else's problem.

"Runner north to south!" Sarah called. "It's Pike."

"Visual," Carter grunted. "Deputy Morales—"

"I see him," Morales said. "He looks like regret."

Pike hit the access and shouldered into a cop-shaped wall. Morales took the angle well, pushed him sideways into the dune face, and made gravity her deputy. The sound it made was not cinematic. It was chalk on asphalt, tires on shell, air leaving a chest too fast.

Pike's hand went for his waistband and found a magnet license frame instead of a pistol. Morales bent his wrist and spoke a sentence that knocked the fight out of him without asking for a second clause.

"Advised," Carter said, already vaulting the last rail toward the south lot.

On the bar, the stuck skiff tried to undrown itself with noise. The man at the tiller jammed and jammed and jammed again, then threw his weight against a world that has never much cared about men shoving it. Two Coasties stepped onto the flat water like they were walking across their own garage, pushed the bow off the tooth, and let the boat slide into their hands. It is terrifying and beautiful to watch competence at work.

"Two detained," Cam said. "Third is probably listening to me hail him for the fourth time and making poor choices. I love my job."

Back at the north dune, Paws' head snapped toward the sea grape, ears pricked to knife points. He gave one short, soft *woof*—a syllable of fact. Sarah followed his line and found—one more wrong rectangle, smaller and hotter, in the brush itself. Not a lamp this time. A phone, screen bright, light angled down like a wedge. A hand held it. The hand had a manicure that could cut.

The tall woman.

She was crouched, legs coiled, one knee in the sand, her cheek lit by her own treachery. She did not look surprised. She looked...interested.

"Hello," she said softly to the dark, and Paws stopped breathing long enough to make room for the word. Her eyes shifted to him and then to Sarah. "We meet as silhouettes."

"Don't move," Sarah said, and it came out as a favor instead of a command.

The woman smiled like a blade in paper. "I was about to tell you the same thing." Her voice had city in it and court in it and something else—the flint of someone who has never walked into a room unsure of the exits.

She clicked the phone off, and the dark rushed back. "You have a good dog," she said. "He points at things worth seeing."

"You kicked my tripod last night," Sarah said.

The woman's smile went soft, amused. "You have me confused with someone who leaves fingerprints."

"Stay where you are," Anya said from behind the woman, voice low and close, and the tall woman did the math and chose not to test it. Anya's flashlight stayed red. The night held. "Interlace your fingers," Anya said. "Slowly."

The woman did. She did it like a person who could choose a dozen ways to make a simple motion look like you were taking something from her and only one of them made you feel like you were still in charge. She chose the wrong one and somehow made it look right. Anya cuffed her clean, efficient, practiced. The woman didn't flinch. "Watch your head," Anya said as she guided her to stand. "It's valuable."

"I'm flattered you think so," the woman murmured. "What's your dog's name?"

"He answers to *stay*," Sarah said.

The woman turned her head just enough to angle one eye toward Paws. "You've trained him well," she said. "Or he's trained you."

Sophie's hand found Paws' collar and tightened. She wanted to say something brave and perfect; what came out was, "You hurt the babies."

The woman went very, very still. It wasn't guilt. It was interest again, recalibration. "Not directly," she said after a quiet beat. "But if I had...what then?"

"You'd have to answer to all of us," Sophie said, voice clean and bright in the dark, and for a second the tall woman's face flickered with something like approval.

Anya's radio crackled. "Unit on the Tongue," Cam said. "Two suspects detained, vessel secured. One skiff got clever and beached south of the jetty. We have eyes on a gray Tacoma at the south lot with a driver whose blood is mostly caffeine. Deputy Morales?"

"On it," Morales said, and you could hear her grin.

Carter came loping up the access, breath pulled tight into the job. He took in the cuffs, the woman, the way Anya held the space with her body and her deep caution. He nodded to Paws—two fingers, thanks—and addressed the woman like he was confirming a reservation. "Evening. I'm Ben Carter. You are under arrest for—well, we'll fill in the line breaks in a minute. Would you like to tell me your name or are we going to name you after your shoes?"

She looked down at her boots as if they had asked to be included in the conversation. They were black and quiet and expensive. "You can call me whatever the paperwork enjoys," she said. "It doesn't change what I am."

"And that is?" Carter asked.

"A lawyer," she said, and smiled with the part of her mouth that smiles in court when she has asked a question she knows the answer to. "Which is why you should be very careful what you decide to do with my phone."

"We won't decide anything without a warrant," Carter said. "We may be excitable, but we are not sloppy."

"You are both," she said gracefully. "But tonight you are less sloppy than excitable. Congratulations."

Cam's voice, to the rescue: "Heads up at Command. We've got more than we planned for. Two unmarked drums just rolled off a tailgate half a mile south of you. They're leaking something that looks like money if money were oily. County, I need a pickup with a soul and a spill kit."

Mark felt his stomach find gravity and grab it with both hands. "Spill kit here," he said into the radio. "We're rolling."

"Negative, civilians stay put," Carter snapped, then swallowed the reflex and rewired it. "Mark—you can stage the kit at the tape. County will take it from there. Sarah—you and the dog stay exactly where you are."

A second later: "Please," he added, because he'd learned a new language in the last week and it had the same words but in a different order.

The south lot took on siren color. Deputy Morales' voice cut through: "Driver of the Tacoma, out of the vehicle, hands where I can see them. That's a beautiful aftermarket bar. Shame if it had to be inventory."

The driver—Brandon Pike's buddy, from his height and his sarcasm—chose the worst possible sentence: "You can't—" and then discovered that yes, in fact, they could.

The Tongue quieted. The lantern on the stick guttered and died under a Coast Guard boot. The generator hum bled down to a sulk and then to silence. The ocean got its own voice back and used it.

The drums in the south lot bled a slick line under the tailgate—a ribbon that caught the red-blue, turned it into a horror movie. The smell hit the wind. Paws recoiled, sneezed twice, then shoved his face into Sarah's leg as if to wipe the stink off his world.

"Don't touch it," Anya said into the radio. "Photograph, cordon, booms if you have them. No one breathes that in for free."

"We have booms," came a new voice—Tac Fire. "We'll earn our keep tonight."

Silas took the long way around the command post and set his palm flat on the drift fence, as if asking permission of something older than any of them. He looked at Mark, then at the water, then at the woman in cuffs. "This isn't their end," he said softly. "This is a finger off a hand."

Carter angled the tall woman toward the path with careful, unfriendly care. "You want to tell me about the rest of the hand?" he asked, conversational.

"Discovery is a wonderful process," she said. "You'll enjoy it. Your dog will enjoy it more."

She paused, almost imperceptibly, looked south toward the cove beyond the jetty where Heron's Cove nested in its own black. "If you're smart," she said so low only Sarah caught it, "you'll look where the water looks slow."

"What does that mean?" Sarah asked, and the woman smiled like a person passing a secret in a crowded train—something kind because it had nothing to do with mercy and everything to do with appetite.

"It means I'm bored by this level of chess," she murmured. "Bring me something with more boards."

"Enough," Carter said, and took her away.

The next hour was a hive that had learned to hum in one key. The detained skiff disgorged its nonsense: coils of monofilament with taped hooks, two portable halogens, a bundle wrapped in blue plastic with 184 inked on it three times like you could write truth into a lie if you just repeated it enough. A Coastie held it up like a dead snake. "You want this on your chain, Ranger, or you want me to make Cam sleep with it?"

Anya's gloved hands took it as if it were the delicate heart of a wrong machine. "You bag it," she said. "You sign it. Then you hand it to me and I sign it and hand it to Carter and he signs it. Nobody breathes on it overly."

County firefighters laid booms and kitty litter around the two drums in the lot like a rosary. The drums themselves got bagged—a whole new level of zip. The leaking didn't smell like diesel. It smelled like a lab that didn't have windows. Sarah watched the wind blow it away from the drains and imagined turtles nosing that slick, reading it the way they read the world—and made herself stop imagining anything she couldn't put on a stand.

The KIDS' CORNER turned into triage for attention spans. Mrs. Gable told a story about loggerheads that made even volunteer cops breathe slower.

At the north dune, Paws lay down like the floor knew his shape and stayed. Twice he got up because the night got a thought; twice Sarah laid him back down with her hand and a word. The second time he went heavy and breathed through his nose until the world unrolled again.

Sophie watched, hands fisted in the hem of her shirt, feet making prints she then erased with the side of her shoe. "How long do we have to be boring," she whispered, as if the night had ears and a sense of humor.

"Until boring turns into leverage," Sarah said, and then flinched because it sounded like Ben.

"Until boring wins," Sophie corrected, and stuck a turtle sticker to Paws' harness as if it were a medal. He accepted it like a man accepts an honor he already knows he deserves.

By midnight the edges had blurred. Paper had been signed, carried, countersigned. Pike had been loaded, cursing blandly with the small vocabulary of a tired coward. The tall woman had been driven away upright, gaze forward, mouth not smiling because that would have given too much to an audience she didn't respect.

Cam came onto the local channel just to say, "All vessels clear. Polaris heading back out for a last look. Flir shows one cold spot under the jetty that looks like a fridge glued to the bottom of the world. If anybody asks, I didn't see that because if I saw that I'd be curious and we don't indulge my curiosity after midnight."

Anya rolled her shoulders, neck popping once. She looked ten years older and five pounds lighter. "We got them on the bar," she said to Carter in a voice that did not allow the word *good* to be used yet. "We have drums, a bundle, fish line, and Pike."

"We don't have the boat," Carter said, equally grim. "We don't have the hand. We have a thumb and two fingers and an attitude."

Silas tapped the map. "Heard your tall girl," he said. "Slow water. That cove."

"Heron's," Sarah said. The name tasted like memory—like the night a boat's belly opened there, like oily residue on a box, like a turtle shell scar. "They use the Tongue as theater. They work the cove quiet."

Paws got up and stretched—forelegs long, hips high, the stretch that resets a dog's night. He turned toward the cove. He stood like a statue made by someone who only carved things that loved.

"Cam," Anya said, back on the radio, voice writing a new sentence, "run me a thermal sweep over Heron's Cove. Low and slow. No lights. Tell me if the water's holding its breath."

Cam went quiet for a count of twenty that felt like longer. "You didn't hear this," he said when he came back, "because my fuel budget doesn't like me at this hour. But if you had heard, you would have heard me say there's a heat puddle tucked under the western bulkhead that shouldn't be there at this tide. Could be a manatee. Could be the refrigerator we weren't discussing. Could be nothing. Could be everything."

Carter looked at Anya. Anya looked at the ocean. Sarah looked at Paws, who did not look at her. He looked at the line where dark water turned darker and told them something none of them could read and all of them felt.

"We don't go tonight," Carter said, and hated himself for being the voice of the law in a world that wanted justice with its hands. "We would be sloppy. We have enough to get the next paper. We go tomorrow. We go with a warrant and a camera and a lot of boring."

"Boring wins," Anya said, giving the words back the dignity they demand. "We sleep three hours. We meet at five. We hit the cove with the sun."

Sophie sagged like a kite when the wind quits. "Tomorrow?" she asked, because tomorrow is a big word for a kid who has learned a lot about the size of nights.

"Tomorrow," Sarah said, and kissed her hair gritty with blown sand. "We had a job tonight and we did it. Now we do the next one."

Mrs. Gable materialized with cocoa that tasted like childhood and command decisions. "If boring is winning," she said tartly, "then cocoa is strategy."

Silas tugged his cap down to his eyebrows. "You all go home," he said. "I'll sit with the ghosts. I like it when they think I'm expected."

"Don't be a hero," Anya told him automatically.

"Never," he said mildly. "I only curate them."

They broke down the command post in the same neat hurry with which they'd built it—evidence inside, hopes folded, anger zipped. The red porch light at the Reynolds' house had burned all night and would burn until dawn. Sophie sleepwalked the last half block with Paws' leash looped in her elbow and her head on his shoulder. Paws took slow, careful steps like he was carrying glass.

At the door, the world made a small noise. A text landed on Sarah's phone like a pebble in a still pool. You're predictable. No number, no name. The syntax like the tall woman's, or like any woman who has used this sentence to win a hearing.

Sarah typed, So are tides. She didn't hit send. She let the reply sit there and warm the glass.

In the small hours, the beach slept, and some of the people who loved it pretended to. At 03:12 a fog rolled in like a thief in socks and sat on the cove like it owned it. Paws' ears lifted; he made a sound so low it wasn't a sound, and Sarah's hand found his scruff in the dark because it always would. He didn't get up. He didn't need to. He knew the difference between *now* and *next*.

When dawn finally ghosted the windows, the ocean looked like it had forgiven everything. It hadn't. It had filed it. The warrants were printed and waiting in a manila folder on Carter's front seat. The coffee had learned to stand up on its own legs. The map had new circles on it like targets and prayers.

At the edge of town, a gray Tacoma sat under a salt-pinched pine, magnet frame back on its plate, hood ticking a slow metronome. Somewhere close by, a flat-bottom boat with a hold built for wrong things took on a shallow breath and decided it would not be there when the sun got its act together.

"Five o'clock," Anya said into the radio, not bothering to keep the hope out of her voice. "Meet at the cove. Bring your patience. Bring your boring. Bring your dog."

Paws stood at the door as if the command had found him first. He looked at the horizon like something had written on it. His tail thumped once—low, deliberate.

"Okay," Sarah said to the day, to the dog, to herself. "Okay. We're in it. We do this right."

"Next one's the hand," Silas had said.

"Next one's the boat," Carter had said.

Paws said nothing. He didn't have to. The bar was drawn tight. The line held. The hook was set. And somewhere under slow water, something that thought it knew all the ways out of a place was about to meet people who had learned to make the truth louder and the boring beautiful.

Chapter 6
NIGHT OF FALSE LIGHTS

By dusk the heat broke, but not the tension. The porch still smelled faintly of bleach from the fish and the note—STAY IN YOUR LANE—they'd bagged for Carter. Mark had tightened every hinge on the doors as if torque could pass for control. Sarah had checked batteries twice, then checked the impulse to check a third time. Paws paced a tight figure eight between the threshold and the top step, glancing at the red porch bulbs as if they, too, were on duty.

"We can rotate," Sarah said, zipping the field pack. "Two hours on the north flats, then we trade. You and Silas take the first watch. I'll sit the dunes with Sophie."

Mark hesitated, half a heartbeat, then nodded. "We stick to the plan. We call first. We don't improvise."

"Boring builds cases," Sarah echoed, and if her voice was steady it was because she'd taught it how to be.

Sophie appeared in the doorway like a question mark with a braid. Her red headlamp filter dangled from its elastic. Paws stepped backward so their shoulders touched—habit, ritual, promise.

"You remember the rules," Sarah said, crouching so they were eye-to-eye. "You stay within arm's reach. You keep the beam low. If I say we leave, we leave."

Sophie drew herself up and saluted with two fingers like she'd seen Anya do. "Yes, ma'am."

Leo shuffled in, pajama pants twisted, hair a warning flare. "Can I—"

"You can help tomorrow at dawn," Mark said gently. "Today is for boring."

Leo scowled. "I can be boring."

"You're a force of nature," Sarah said, kissing his forehead. "For now, guard the sofa."

Silas honked twice from the street—his truck's horn a bass note that somehow never woke anyone who didn't need waking. He leaned out the window with a thermos thick enough to be a bludgeon. "You coming to sit with the ghosts?" he called to Mark.

"Only one of us is the ghost," Mark said, hefting the binoculars. "Let's go watch the stars."

The north flats wore their usual twilight—low wind, damp sand throwing back the last light like a secret. Far offshore, the Coast Guard cutter Polaris sat in silhouette, lights blacked out to a bruise. Closer in, a skiff traced a slow, cautious path across the Serpent's Tongue, never committing, never trusting the water beyond the next ripple.

Silas parked at the turnout and killed the engine. They sat in the thickening dark, windows cracked, listening to the sound a restless ocean makes when it's trying to be patient.

"You ever think about leaving?" Mark asked, and surprised himself by how much it sounded like he was asking the beach.

"Sometimes," Silas said. "But then I remember that anywhere else I go is still going to have men who think the rules are for other men."

"It's the smiley face," Mark said, and Silas snorted.

"Smiley face was the tell," he agreed. "Boys who've never had to hide think a joke makes them invisible."

At 21:06, a pair of dim taillights slid down the south access road like a pair of eyelids toward sleep. The vehicle stopped by the last trash barrel. No doors opened. The taillights pulsed once, twice—somebody's private code.

Silas checked his watch. "Half an hour to low," he murmured. "They'll set up while the water falls."

Mark texted Sarah: Activity at south access. Red-only. Stick to plan. Three dots bloomed and vanished. Then: Copy. In position at E-7. Paws alert but quiet. He pictured them against the dune line, the discipline in the line of Sophie's back, Paws' weight distributed forward onto his toes, every sense lit.

Silas drank from the thermos. "We wait," he said. "And we do not get cute."

On the east dunes, the night changed. It started as a smell—sweet and wrong, like warm plastic and penny-iron—and then as a sound, a thin metallic hum hiding under the bow wave of the surf. Paws stopped moving. He lifted his head and drew air over his palate in a long, deliberate pull; his ears tipped forward. He looked at Sarah, then at the dark spine of dune to their right.

Sophie angled her beam low and slow, the red light knitting bars of shadow and glow across the sand. "What is it, boy?" she whispered.

The hum got louder, resolved into a generator whine somewhere inland. Then—slice—an electric glare bled through the sea oats, a rectangle of raw, white light stabbing the night. Another rectangle winked on, fifty yards south. A third banged alive by the cut at E-7. The beach flinched.

"Kill lights," Sarah said softly, and they did. Their own darkness felt like a cloak.

The white rectangles weren't floodlights in any true sense; they were portable work lamps on tripods, the kind you set up to paint a garage at midnight. But here, they were wrongness made visible. Against the bright, the black dunes became void; the surf slid out of sight; the horizon died.

"False lights," Sarah said, bile high. "They're trying to pull hatchlings inland."

A sound answered her—a faint scritching from the upland nest where the ranger stake read N-12. The sand trembled under a scatter of tiny claws. Sophie clapped a hand to her mouth. "They're boiling," she breathed.

At the base of the nearest tripod, a cheap extension cord ran into the grass, then into the dune, snakeskin orange against the sand. The hiss of the generator spiked—the sound of something under load. Paws rumbled, the sound deep and contained; he looked at Sarah, then took one step toward the nearest light and stopped when she didn't move.

"Photograph first," Sarah said. She lifted her phone and shot one quick frame, then another of the cord and its route. She wanted to smash the tripod. She took photos instead.

Her radio burred softly against her shoulder. Anya's voice came small and compressed across the channel. "Unit Seven to beach. Reports of false lighting at E-7 and south. Rangers en route. Everyone who is not a ranger does not touch. Over."

"Copy," Sarah whispered, even though whispering didn't change the physics of radio. She keyed to a second channel. "Mark, false lights at E-7, south, and mid. Hatchlings starting to boil at N-12. Anya is on her way."

Three dots, then: Hold. Photograph. I'm coming from north with Silas. He added, because he knew her too well: We will smash them *later*.

A movement inland—two figures shouldering through the sea grape, black against bright, each carrying a canvas bag that sagged with weight. One of them wore a brimmed cap, flat and cocky. Even from this distance, the body language read like Brandon Pike.

Sophie's breath hitched. Paws leaned into her knee like a promise and held.

The men stopped by the tripod, checked the cord and the angle, then cut south toward the next light, laughing like men in dark bars. Sarah watched the way their feet fell, the way they used the dune's shoulder to hide their silhouettes from the water. They knew their way.

"Record, not intervene," she told herself. "Record."

Behind them, the scritching at N-12 went from rumor to chorus. Sand shivered. The nest pocked, then broke. Thirty, forty, fifty dark commas burst from the crater and ran upslope toward the glare. In that first frantic minute, instinct and wrongness fought; instinct lost to the lie of light.

Sarah swore under her breath. "Okay," she said to no one and to everyone. She unrolled the dark cloth panel from her pack, snapped it open, and handed one end to Sophie. "Barrier. Low and gentle. Don't pick them up unless they're trapped. We guide with shadow. Paws—*stay*."

Paws lay down so fast it was as if gravity had pointed out an option. His eyes didn't leave the nest. His tail didn't move. His whole body said, *here*.

They set the cloth like a fence between the boil and the false lights, a black river the hatchlings ran into and along. The tiny bodies hesitated, reoriented, swung left toward the real horizon—the long, honest brightness above the waterline. Two stragglers flailed in a scrap of ghost net; Sophie knelt and freed them with careful fingers, whispering apologies to the night. One hatchling marched onto Paws' front paw; he didn't flinch.

A hatchling made a wrong turn toward the generator's thrum, caught in the seam between cloth and sand; Sophie cupped her hands and made a tunnel of shade. It worked. The baby turned, slid into her shadow, and made for the sea as if it had made the choice itself.

Over the radio came Ben Carter's voice, the sound of a man walking faster than he'd planned. "South unit walking in. Anya five minutes out. Cam off Polaris in ten. Eyes on, hands off, please, until—"

"Until the beach is on fire?" Sarah muttered, then into the radio: "Copy, but we have a boil and false lights. We're guiding without touching."

"That is—under the present circumstances—acceptable," Carter said, which in Ben-speak was something like *thank you for doing the right thing just this once before I got here.*

In the glare 200 yards south, Pike and his partner knelt at the second tripod. They weren't in a hurry. They worked with the self-regard of people who think the world will bend. One of them held up a hand light and painted it lazily over the dune grass. Hatchlings ran toward it like iron filings toward a magnet.

Mark's text popped: Silas and I are eighty meters north of you, behind the fence line. We've got eyes on Pike. County unit is on the access road. Do not move.

As if in answer, a third figure appeared near the first tripod—another bag over a shoulder, but smaller, taller, moving like she wore her certainty like a suit. Lila from Doran? No. Even in silhouette this woman carried herself like she'd have you sign something before she punched you. She knelt, did something at the generator—probably nothing more technical than kicking it to quiet a hiccup—and stood, looking straight down the dune line toward where Sarah crouched in the dark.

The woman lifted a hand, casual. The gesture said, *I see you. And what?* Then she turned and followed Pike.

Sophie's nails dug crescents into the cloth. "They know we're here," she whispered.

"They don't know who we are," Sarah said. "And they do not know that Ben is the color of fury right now."

A new sound: tires biting shell up on the access. Carter's radio voice escalated half a notch. "County unit at the south gate. All parties sit tight." A pause and then, lower, for the officers: "Do not light them up until they're at the vehicle. I want the vehicle."

The last of the hatchlings hit the wash and vanished as if swallowed by a kinder darkness. Sarah exhaled a breath she didn't know she'd been rationing. "Go," she whispered to the ocean, because it had things to do.

At the second tripod, Pike straightened and slung the empty bag over his shoulder. His partner shouldered the other. They started up the dune, cutting a high line so their footprints wouldn't show where they shouldn't. The tall woman lingered a heartbeat, pivoted, walked south toward the third light alone.

"Mark?" Sarah whispered into the radio. "Three targets. Two northbound with bags. One southbound. Who's closer?"

"Copy. I have the two in my window. Tall one is yours if you have to choose." Silas' voice came from behind the words. "Your tall girl walks like a boss. She'll make our lives interesting."

"Understood," Sarah said.

Carter again, taut now: "County unit rolling. All observers hold. Repeat: hold."

The county SUV slid into view at the access. Lights off. Hood low. Carter and a deputy hopped out, small and dark in all that wrong light. Carter moved like deliberate gravity; the deputy moved like coffee. They eased along the dune line, using the floodlit shadows as cover the way you use cover you hate: thoroughly.

Pike and his partner crested the dune shoulder and dropped toward the access path. Carter let them come, let them get cocky, let them get almost to the trash barrel before he stepped out and said conversationally, "Evening, gents."

Everything happened at once. Pike flinched, then tried to smile, then tried to bolt, all in one bad sentence. The partner went for his waistband and found nothing helpful. Carter didn't draw—he was too close and too good. He grabbed the partner's arm, turned, levered, and the man met the sand with a thud that carried the weight of training. The deputy moved on Pike. Pike threw sand like a playground bully and sprinted for the truck.

"Plate!" Sophie hissed, needless and urgent.

"Eight-three," Mark said calmly into the radio. "Fish cover. Gray Tacoma. Aftermarket bars. 184 sticker on the bumper."

The Tacoma's engine barked. The truck lurched, wheels spinning, spitting shell. The deputy grabbed for the door, missed. The truck fishtailed, clipped the tripod, took the light down with a satisfying crash that made the world a little more right, then barreled up the access.

"County to all," the deputy yelled into his shoulder as he ran. "Vehicle fleeing southbound. Plate obscured. Driver known. Officer in foot pursuit. Send me something with sirens."

South down the tide line, the tall woman didn't run. She turned her walk into a saunter, as if none of this touched her, as if the beach were a runway and she owned it. She reached the third tripod, kicked its legs in with a clean, efficient motion, and dropped the generator choke. The light died. She stood there in the new dark, letting her eyes adjust, as if she might see who else shared it.

She looked north once more and lifted two fingers—the same casual salute Sophie had given Sarah earlier. Then she stepped into the sea grape and disappeared like a good idea.

"Whoever she is," Sarah murmured, "she knows how to leave prints without leaving prints."

"Anya's going to hate that sentence," Mark said in her ear.

Sirens yawled far inland, then closer, then cut; red and blue flickered low behind the dune line, painting the sea oats like a cheap bar. Cam's voice crackled from the marine band—a separate radio in the pack. "Polaris has eyes on a pickup running south on the coastal road without lights, speed forty. Request county unit at mile 12."

"Copy," Carter said, breathing harder now. "Suspect vehicle is gray Tacoma with vanity fish frame and partial 83. Second suspect in custody. Third unknown female last seen on foot near E-7."

"Unknown female?" Anya asked from somewhere north of the beach, and if sarcasm could cut tape, they wouldn't need scissors. "Unit Seven en route E-7. Whoever is on the dune with a dog, back ten yards."

"We're already back," Sarah said. "Hatchlings are clear. We have photographs of the lights and cords. Paws held."

"Tell him he gets an extra biscuit," Anya said, and that was as close to *good job* as a ranger got when the night still had calories in it.

By the time Carter walked the bagged partner past the N-12 stake, the beach had exhaled. The generator's hum went to silence. The tripods lay like dead insects. The ocean resumed its old, honest conversation with the moon.

The partner kept his chin high. He had sand in his hair and a grin that tried to land somewhere between defiance and charm. It landed on *expired warranty*. Carter didn't look at him. He looked at the canvas bag the deputy carried in two gloved hands like a heart.

"We'll open it at the truck," Carter said, which again was Ben-speak for *I'd like to open it now but I like my job*.

"Photographs," Sarah reminded herself, and took three more.

Anya arrived with two rangers, all three of them wearing the faces of people who were going to stay mad until they were certain it would be useful not to be. She looked at the tripod leg, at the scoured patch of sand where Pike's tire had spun, at the generator's makeshift choke, at the hatchling tracks pointed the wrong way and then righted. She looked at Paws, who looked back with the flat calm of a dog who'd done a thing and didn't need it named.

"Good hold," she told him, and then to Sarah: "I owe you a lecture about hands off. I'll give it in the morning. For now, thank you for letting them go to sea."

Carter called out, "Open the bag," and everyone, being human, looked.

The deputy slit the canvas and peeled it back. Inside: coil upon coil of monofilament line, hooks taped every yard with neat, surgical care; four headlamps without red filters; three portable work lights identical to the dead ones; and a vacuum-sealed bundle the size of a paperback book, wrapped in blue plastic with 184 inked on one side. The bundle smelled like solvent and money.

Carter didn't swear. He didn't smile either. "Photograph," he said to the deputy, who did, and then, to the partner: "You want to tell me which end of this you think is the safe one?"

The man shrugged. "Found it."

"Classic," Carter said for the third time in two days, and motioned the deputy to bag the bundle again.

A ranger jogged in from the south, breath white in the headlamp. "We found the generator's hide," she reported, lifting a mesh camo tarp with pride. "And a box of halogens. Also this." She held up a spiral notebook in a zip bag—the sort you buy at a gas station when you realize courts prefer paper to memory. The cover had an oil thumbprint like a signature.

"Don't open it," Carter said, sharp. "Bag, tag, and don't learn to read until I have a warrant."

"That woman," Sarah said. "The tall one. She kicked the tripod clean. She knew what she was doing."

Anya looked past her at the dark south, where the dune fell away to the cut. "We'll get her on the next pass," she said. "People like that don't come out for a trial run and then retire."

Silas appeared out of the dark like a ghost you'd hired as a guide. He handed Carter a flat, gray rectangle. "Magnet from your boy's plate," he said. "It and I had words at the cattle gate before he remembered he didn't want it anymore." He scratched the dog behind the ear. "You held."

Paws sighed, which might have meant, *We're tired of holding,* or *We will hold again.*

By two a.m., the lights were down, the generators loaded, the evidence logged and the angry packed away, at least publicly. Carter took the partner up the access in quiet cuffs. The county unit idled, waiting to take the bag, the notebook, the 184-stamped rectangle of blue. Cam, still a voice more than a person to most of them, reported Polaris had tracked the Tacoma until it ducked into streets with names and too many places to hide. "We'll see him again," Cam said, and nobody argued.

Sarah and Sophie walked the last fifty yards of hatchling tracks to the wrack line and stood with their toes at the foam, letting the simple, ear-level hiss erase the generator's whine. Sophie wiped her face with the back of her hand and was surprised to find tears. "Sorry," she said, reflexive.

"For what?" Sarah asked.

"For... being mad," Sophie said. "For wanting to tear all the lights down."

Sarah pressed a palm to her back. "That wasn't anger that wanted to smash the lights," she said. "That was love."

Sophie nodded, and the nod was an older one than it had been an hour before.

Behind them, Anya's voice carried, softer now. "I know you want to smash things," she told someone too far away to see. "But the boring is what holds. You smash in your head; you photograph in your hands."

Silas stood at the dune foot like a weathered post. He looked at the tracks, at the flat blackness that was the real horizon. "Old men used to leave a lantern on the bar to bring boats in," he said. "Some of 'em did it to drown their neighbors for insurance. People been lying with light a long time." He spit neatly into the foam. "We'll be meaner than they are. We'll be patient."

They got home to quiet. No fish on the steps. No note. Only the red light and a bucket of clean water for boots and a dog asleep before his harness was fully off.

Mark unclipped the OBSERVER badge and set it on the mantel. He wasn't sure if it looked noble or ridiculous. He was sure he didn't care.

Sarah pulled the zip bag with the notebook out of her pack and slid it into a larger evidence envelope. Her hands shook just enough to remind her they were hers. She wrote Recovered south beach, near E-7, prox tripod 3 in neat, measured letters down the margin. "Chain of custody," she whispered to herself.

"Chain of custody is boring." She set it next to the 184 rectangle, next to the photo of the drum. Puzzle pieces. Edges first. Then the picture.

Her phone buzzed. A text from a number she didn't have saved: You did good work tonight. Stop before it stops being yours.

No name. No signature emoji. The syntax felt female. The sentence felt like a dare.

She forwarded it to Carter. Unknown female. Likely our tripod kicker. Then wrote: We stop when you say we stop.

His reply came back in two bubbles. I never say stop. I say stay behind the tape.

She smiled despite the sand in her teeth. Boring builds cases.

Now you're getting it, he wrote.

In the tiny hours, when the house held its breath, Mark lay awake staring at the ceiling and counted the ways this could go wrong. He got to forty-three and stopped because he didn't like the shape of forty-four.

Beside the bed, Paws' breathing went slow and deep. The dog snored once, a harmless, human sound. Something in Mark's chest let go.

"We're in it," he said into the dark.

"We're in it," Sarah agreed, already halfway to asleep. "And we're not in it alone."

Morning was a pale rumor at the windows when the doorbell rang like a doorbell had never had to be quiet in its life. On the porch stood Ben Carter in yesterday's shirt, two coffees, and a smile that was mostly teeth.

"Judge woke up cranky," he said, stepping in without waiting. "Signed off anyway. We've got warrants for three sheds, two boats, and one house with a very ugly couch. Also, we ran your 184 tag through three databases and at least one bad memory. It's... showing up."

"Where?" Mark asked.

"On shipping manifests that never made the shipping part," Carter said. "On fuel orders paid cash. On a lobster pot registry that swears the number belongs to a woman who died in 2004. On a dive chart misfiled as a bingo card. It's almost like someone wanted a number to mean more than one thing, which I love as a person who enjoys unraveling threads and hate as a man who wants to sleep."

Anya appeared behind him, hair damp, uniform crisp, eyes lit. She held up a photo—satellite image, grainy but clear enough. Two small boats at anchor near the Serpent's Tongue. A line of boxes laid out along a sandbar like piano keys. Men the size of punctuation moving among them.

"Tonight wasn't random," she said. "Tonight was rehearsal."

Silas, who had apparently decided their kitchen was now a wharf, lifted his thermos in salute. "Told you," he said. "Men who think they're clever like to practice what they're going to brag about later."

"Here's the plan," Anya said, laying out a map on the table, coffee ring landing on the legend. "We take your photographs and your notebook and your fish note and your 184 and we walk it to the DA. We get a green light to sit a net over the Tongue. Polaris outside, county at both access roads, rangers on the dune, volunteers—" She looked at Sarah and Mark. "—inside, behind tape, with radios, doing the boring work."

Sophie slid into a chair, hair an explosion, eyes already bright. "And me?" she asked.

"And you," Anya said, smiling her rare, quick smile, "get to help Mrs. Gable set up a kids' table next to the command post so she can keep all your parents from biting their nails off. Because when this goes, it's going to go fast."

"How fast?" Mark asked.

Carter sipped coffee, grimaced like it had lied to him, and said, "Fast like boats choose bad water if they think the cut is clear. Fast like trucks think tape is decoration. Fast like men with smiley faces on their cards learn to frown."

Sarah looked at the red porch light still glowing faint against morning and thought of hatchlings turning toward what lied to them and then back toward what was true. "Then we make the truth louder," she said.

"And we keep the lights red," Sophie added, with the absolute certainty of a child who had guided something small to something vast and won.

Paws thumped his tail once, a single, low drumbeat against the floor. He looked at the door like a dog who understood that sometimes the world you love asks you to sit, and sometimes it asks you to go.

"Tonight," Anya said, tapping the map, voice steady, eyes sharp. "We make our lane the lane. And we make anyone who tries to drive through it regret that choice."

No one cheered. No one had energy for that. They nodded, counted radios, stacked batteries, packed field cloths and extra vials and Paws' collapsible bowl. They wrote timings in the margins of a map already tattooed with other men's estimates. They texted neighbors. They kissed their kids. They set the porch light to red before the sun had fully remembered how to rise.

The day stretched long and taut, like a line strung between posts. The ocean breathed in and out. Somewhere in town, Brandon Pike found a new magnet frame for his plate. Somewhere else, the tall woman with the clean kick bought a coffee and didn't look at the morning paper. Out beyond the bar, Polaris idled and watched the horizon like it might try something.

And Paws slept, then woke, then slept again, conserving a dog's patient courage for the hour when the lights would lie and the beach would need everyone who loved it to tell the truth loudly, and in sequence, and without blinking.

Chapter 7
UNMASKING THE VILLAINS

The engine's snarl dwindled into the storm's relentless percussion, leaving a taut stillness on the beach. Mark kept his arm around Sophie as they watched the grey horizon swallow the dark hull. Sarah swept the shoreline with her gaze, as if she could erase the boat's shadow by sheer force of will. Paws paced three strides toward the surf and held there, ears up, listening.

"They're gone," Sarah said, voice rough. "For now."

Mark nodded but didn't look away. "Lucky," he said, then pointed. "And careless."

A slab of netting had snagged on a tooth of rock where the boat had faltered—heavy, weed-slick, and wrong. The three of them crossed the sloping sand, Paws falling in at Mark's heel. Up close, the netting was industrial and intentional: thick cords, reinforced lines, sections of finer mesh nested inside the broader weave. Not flotsam—equipment.

"This has been riding the current awhile," Sarah murmured, tugging; it wouldn't budge.

Mark felt along the wet knots and stopped. Beneath the tangle his glove brushed something rigid and smooth. He worked without speaking, teasing cords aside until the net yielded a dark, box-shaped seam—stitched in so cleverly it vanished unless you knew to look.

He slid the waterproof compartment free. Inside, sealed bags lay cushioned on shredded plastic. He opened one and his breath hitched: a tiny seahorse, opal-pale, curled and impossibly delicate. Another bag held a fan of living coral; a third, small anemones, their tentacles quivering even out of water; another, a glassy-eyed juvenile fish.

"What are they?" Sophie whispered.

"Rare," Mark said softly. "And stolen." He met Sarah's eyes. "This isn't dumping. It's trafficking."

Anger rose in Sarah, hot and clean. The seahorse looked like a charm plucked from a child's dream and pinned to a ledger. The coral's architecture—centuries written in calcium—reduced to inventory.

"They're selling them," she said, the words tasting bitter. "Collectors. Black market."

Mark resealed the bags and examined the work with a grim reverence. The stitching on the hidden pocket was waterproofed and tight; the mesh varied by square inch to sort by size; the bag seals were oxygenated. "They planned for transit," he said. "This net is dual-use—catcher and courier."

He turned the heavy webbing, reading its logic the way he'd read the map: denser knots here for small specimens; stronger lines there for larger stock; reinforced tie-points that matched the pocket's anchor seams. He pictured the assembly, the forethought, the cost—and how many times they'd run it before.

Sophie squeezed Sarah's hand. "What happens to them now?"

"We get them to people who can help," Mark said, knowing the odds and refusing them anyway. "We'll do it right."

He secured the compartment back into the net so it wouldn't tear loose in transit, then heaved the whole mass onto his shoulder. As he did, something flashed dully inside the cords. He fished out a tarnished silver charm: a dolphin, small and unassuming.

"What is it?" Sarah asked.

"Someone's token," Mark said, slipping it into his pocket. "Ironic, isn't it?"

They started the slow trudge up-beach with the evidence between them. Paws ranged ahead, nose working, then veered toward a cluster of tide-worn rocks. He nudged, paused, and picked up a single waterproof glove with unusual care. Back with the group, he dropped it at Sophie's feet and thumped the sand with his tail.

Sophie crouched. An embroidered logo, faint beneath the grit, caught the light: a wave braided through an anchor in a distinctive blue.

"I know this," she blurted. "The Salty Dog—down by the harbor. The shop with the coils of rope stacked like towers. It's their logo."

The name clicked into place for all three at once. The Salty Dog was a local fixture—reputable, friendly, the place you went for gear and gossip.

Paws nudged Sophie's wrist, then flicked a look toward the line of coves where the boat had vanished. A breadcrumb, and he wanted them to see it as such.

Mark slid the glove into one of the waterproof bags. "If they're sourcing here, they're local—or someone in town is feeding them."

"Or both," Sarah said, thinking aloud. "Special orders, reinforced net, pocket materials, dive gear. If those purchases exist, someone sold them—and kept records."

"We can't walk in and point fingers," Mark cautioned. "But with this—" he patted the net "—and the glove, we have more than a story."

They pushed on, the storm easing to a harsh drizzle that slicked the sand like poured lead. The weight of the net bit into Mark's shoulder; Sarah steadied the drag with both hands. Sophie carried the waterproof box of rescued animals like a treasure chest, eyes fixed, steps sure. Paws stayed close to her leg, a steadying presence.

"They use weather as cover," Mark said between breaths. "Low visibility, no patrols. And small sabotage—trash, broken nests—to keep curious people away."

Sarah nodded. "Drive off witnesses, control the shoreline, harvest what they want." She looked at the box in Sophie's hands. "It's organized, not sloppy."

They reached the dune path. Mark lowered the net, breath steaming in the cool air. The evidence lay there—weight, seam, logic—no longer whispers in the dark. He photographed everything: the pocket, the seals, the mesh, the serial pattern of the knotwork.

Sarah labeled the glove bag and took a close shot of the logo. Sophie, trembling only a little, photographed the seahorse.

Paws stood with his chest lifted and his nose to the wind as if taking attendance of every threat and every ally on the beach.

"We go two ways," Sarah said, settling into the plan as if it had been waiting for them. "Immediate triage for these animals—call the rescue center and the marine warden. And a careful look at The Salty Dog's inventory trail, through the right channels."

Mark's jaw eased a fraction. "Rangers first. Let them walk the evidence in. We don't tip our hand to the store—if they're clean, good; if not, let investigators be the surprise."

Sophie looked from the box to the glove to Paws. "Do we tell Mrs. Kwan at the turtle center?" Mrs. Kwan, who knew the tide tables better than the clock.

"We tell her everything," Sarah said. "She knows who to call on the marine side. And we document like mad."

Mark lifted the net again; Sarah took the box from Sophie for a few steps to rest her arms. Paws ranged along the path edge, scanning the scurf of weed, glass, plastic—cataloguing, rejecting.

At the porch, the house felt smaller, the storm louder.

They moved like a team in a field lab: towels down, lights bright, doors latched. Mark spread the net across a tarp and set to cataloging. Sarah phoned the rescue center, voice firm, then the regional warden's office, her notes crisp and complete. Sophie hovered by the sink with a shallow aerated tub and careful hands, listening to instructions, easing the seahorse's bag into a water bath, keeping temperature steady like she'd hold a breath.

Paws lay by the door, alert but finally still, eyes on the world beyond the glass. Every now and then his ears pricked and settled again. Nothing approached.

Mark sealed a final evidence bag and exhaled. "We have names to find," he said, looking to the glove, to the photos, to the map still pinned with its jagged wave marks. "And a store to ask about—quietly."

Sarah touched his shoulder. "We start with what we can save. Then we go after who's taking it."

Sophie leaned into Paws, fingers threading his fur, and he pressed his head into her shoulder as if to say yes—this, and then the rest.

Outside, the storm spent itself against the windows. Inside, the work of unmasking began.

Chapter 6: Unmasking the Villains

"We'll take this straight to Ranger Davies," Mark said, bagging the glove. "Between this and the net, we've got real evidence." He squeezed Sophie's shoulder. "Thanks to you—and Paws."

Sophie hugged the golden fur-friend. "Best detective ever," she whispered. Paws answered with a wag and a whine, pleased, ready.

As they hiked off the beach the storm finally broke, light slicing the cloud deck into ragged silver seams. The glove, stitched with a blue anchor twined in a wave, had turned a night of menace into a pivot. The villains weren't faceless anymore. They had a logo. They had a supply line. And thanks to a dog's nose and a child's recall, the Reynolds had something to follow.

Mark called Brian Davies on the walk back. "Wildlife trafficking," he said, laying out the boat, the net with hidden pockets, the bagged seahorses and coral, and the glove from The Salty Dog. He could hear Brian's disbelief harden into purpose.

"I've heard whispers," Brian said. "Odd netting, unmarked boats at night—nothing we could hold. This changes it. Don't tip anyone off. Meet me with everything—somewhere quiet."

They met that afternoon on a bluff above the recovering sea. Mark handed over the tarped net, the sealed bags, and the glove.

Brian worked like a forensic tech, photographing, labeling, thinking aloud. "Dual-mesh netting. Waterproof pocketry. Oxygenated seals. Not casual poaching—systematized collection." He held the glove up to the light. "If The Salty Dog is complicit—or even just careless—we'll find it in their paper trail. I'll start discreetly."

He sketched a plan: check the shop's recent bulk orders of reinforced netting, rope, and sealants; ask quiet questions of fishermen, patrol staff, and the cliffside birdwatchers who never miss a thing; flag unusual night traffic to the old lighthouse and Black Rock coves; loop in a trusted EPA contact, Dr. Aris Thorne, to prep a formal escalation once evidence stacked.

The next days were a choreography of vigilance and restraint. Mark and Sarah resumed dawn patrols, noticed the sudden lull in debris—less abandon than regrouping, they suspected. Paws patrolled with a rope-tight alertness, pausing to test every breeze. Brian slipped into The Salty Dog as a customer. Arthur Finch—blunt, genial, "reputable"—offered standard nets from the showroom, but Brian clocked industrial spools in back and learned of a recent cash purchase of reinforced rope and waterproof sealant—no receipt, "private project," paid in full. He logged fishermen's whispers, too: rigid, scooplike trawl nets used offshore on moonless nights; small, fast boats pairing with a lumbering mother ship; unfamiliar vans parked by the abandoned lighthouse at odd hours.

Dr. Thorne confirmed parallel reports up the coast—seahorses and specialty corals vanishing from known reefs—but nothing concrete until now. "Your net and that glove let us move," she said. "This setup is professional."

At home, Sophie turned witness into record. Her charcoal pages stitched the night back together: the low, predatory lines of the boat; the reinforced net's mixed mesh; the pocket seams and quick releases; the glove logo, meticulously annotated. She gave Paws his panels, too—ears forward, nose to the sand, pushing the clue toward her hand.

When Mark brought the sketchbook to Brian, the ranger's eyebrows rose. "This is forensic," he said, passing pages to Dr. Thorne. "Angles, integration, function. It explains what text can't." They scanned and logged the drawings alongside photographs and chain-of-custody notes.

"Use them," Mark said. "Use everything."

They would—and sooner than expected.

Twilight stilled the coast to a held breath. Hidden in the dune scrub, Mark and Sophie watched the mouth of a narrow cove while Brian coordinated by whisper in their earpieces. Paws lay at Mark's boot, taut as a bow.

The engine came first: a soft, rhythmic thrum. Paws lifted his head, muscles coiling. "Approaching," Brian murmured. "Do not engage. Observe and report."

A smaller utility boat slid into the shallows and bumped the sand with practiced ease. Two men went to work: one tall and broad-shouldered, the other stocky, directive. A flashlight's beam jittered, carving faces into fragments. Crates moved from boat to shore to a dark van tucked high on the beach.

Sophie's pencil whispered—dimensions, sequence, count. "Heavy, dark wood," she breathed. "He's wearing a cap... can't see—wait. Tattoo on the hand. Looked like a coiled snake."

The light snagged the taller man's profile and something in Mark clicked. The jawline. The set of the eyes. A name swam up from the silt of memory. "Grant," he whispered. "Grant Holloway. Oakhaven Fisheries—laid off before it folded. Big temper. Always railing at regulations."

Brian's reply was immediate. "Holloway's on my radar—volatile, local knowledge, motive. That's a lead."

The men finished, careful and quick. No clatter, no wasted motion. The boat ghosted back into black water; the van rolled off without lights. The cove sealed itself behind them.

"All clear," Brian said at last. "We got what we needed."

They regrouped inland. Grainy night captures from Sophie's phone joined her precise sketches and Mark's identification on Brian's tablet. "This isn't random," Brian said. "It's organized—and personal. Holloway loses a livelihood, blames 'conservation,' and converts expertise into a black-market business. Your 'coiled snake' is an excellent secondary marker, Sophie. We'll cross-reference tattoos and associates."

"What about Finch?" Mark asked. "If Holloway's kitting up—"

"We revisit The Salty Dog," Brian said. "With cause. Your drawings prove specialized net modifications. The glove ties brand to scene. If Finch is clean, he'll help. If he's not, we'll have leverage to look behind the counter."

Sophie nodded, quiet but resolute. "Show him the logo and the net drawings," she said. "Make him answer."

"We will," Brian said. "Carefully."

They walked back under a thin seam of dawn. Sophie leaned against Mark; Paws matched her steps, shoulder brushing her leg like a promise. Fear hadn't left them, but it had changed shape. It had a name now, a face glimpsed in a cutting beam, a tattoo on a working hand, a shop sign by the harbor. The path forward was risky, yes—but visible.

In the kitchen, the house felt smaller and safer all at once. Mark poured water, then turned to Sarah with the recap: the boat, the crates, the van, the name. She listened, jaw set, eyes bright.

"So," she said, "we save what we can save—and we help take the rest down."

Paws lay by the door, ears half-cocked toward the sea. Outside, the tide drew a clean line through the wreckage of the storm. Inside, their case—stitched from a glove, a net, a child's drawings, and a dog's insistence—began to harden into something that could stand up in daylight.

Chapter 8
SLOW WATER

At 04:47, the world belonged to fog and resolve. The parking cutout above Heron's Cove was a smear of dim taillights and people moving like intentions—quiet, clipped, purposeful. Somebody had set a battery lantern on red and slid it under the tailgate of the ranger truck so it bled a low glow across a field table—warrants in a manila stack, tide chart, aerials of the cove laminated and dotted with grease-pencil Xs. Radio checks rasped softly—"check—copy"—the sound of a net tightening.

Anya Sharma's voice cut the hush like a clean knife. "We're on warrants," she said, holding up the signed pages two-fingered as if they were sacramental. "Primary is the fish house and contiguous dock lot at Heron's Cove—address on the doc. Secondary is the cinderblock gear shed by the western bulkhead. Tertiary, if we find cause"—she tapped a third sheet—"is the boathouse at the back inlet. The judge read Donna Vale's arrest report and signed off at 03:19. We serve, we document, we don't freelance."

Carter, jaw tight, nodded to the map. "Land team goes down the north trail—me, Sharma, Alvarez, Keahi. County stays at the gate 'til called. Water team—Silas, you ride herd on our little skiff and hold the mouth. Coast Guard is staging outside the bar. Cam's got FLIR. If it moves hot, he sees it."

Cam's voice came dry and awake over the radio. "Polaris standing by. Fog's a cat. I don't hate it. FLIR loves it."

Mark ran his finger down a checklist: spare gloves, evidence triangles, sterile swabs, amber vials, battery packs, zip ties, camera lenses wiped and ready. He wasn't law. He was the boring part that wins—documentation, chain-of-custody, the relentless refusal to cut corners. Next to the list, Sarah adjusted the strap on her camera and checked the setting that would make her red filter behave like a prayer instead of a blindfold.

Paws leaned into Sarah's shin, anchoring, then exhaled and tested the fog the way he tested a stranger—nose high, a careful draw, a decision behind his eyes. Ozone, wet wood, salt marsh. Under it, threads: solvent sweet, hot plastic, and a faint, reptile-cold chemical he had cataloged last night and decided he didn't like.

Sophie stood at the tailgate with a thermos of cocoa and a sweatshirt two sizes too big that made her look like hope dressed as a kid. Carter bent enough to speak into her eye-line. "You stay with Mrs. Gable at the gate," he said, gentle over steel. "This is a paper morning. Boring. We promise."

"It never is," Sophie said, not unkindly. She stuffed a turtle sticker in the chest pocket of Carter's vest. "For luck."

He looked down, exhaled a half-smile. "I'll take every legal charm I can get."

They moved before dawn could change its mind. The north trail fell away from the lot in a sand-quiet ribbon, the scrub on either side wet with low cloud. Sea grape leaves hung with dew like coins. The cove breathed the colder breath of slow water, and the sound of waves from outside came bent and distant, like a story retold.

"Red only," Anya said, and a handful of thumb-sized beams ghosted into life, aimed at boots, not faces.

Paws slid front, nose mapping in a lattice. The trail kinked left between two wind-buckled cabbage palms, and he stopped fast enough that Sarah's knee kissed his shoulder. The dog's head tilted. He went still, statued into point—paw lifted, tail straight, body a taut wire.

"What have you got?" Sarah whispered.

He eased left three inches, weight shifting toward the palmetto clump, and exhaled through his nose with a soft fff that meant here.

Sarah's beam brushed the sand and found what eyes don't find unless a dog tells them: monofilament strung ankle-high, three treble hooks tied at shin and thigh like someone's idea of a punchline. The fog had beaded on the line so it shimmered like spider-silk. It would have licked a calf and set teeth.

"Hooks," Sarah breathed.

"Copy," Anya said, already down on one knee with trauma shears. "Alvarez, mark and cut. Photo both sides. Bag the line, bag the hooks, label it 'slow trail.' If they did this once, they did it twice. Eyes wide."

They moved again—slower. Twenty yards down, Paws stopped and locked the world a second time. This one sat at chest height, bells wired into it like budget chimes. Keahi clipped, Alvarez bagged. "They want to hear us coming," Carter muttered. "They want our hands bleeding before we open their door."

"They want plausible deniability if a loggerhead dies," Anya said. "Nothing about poaching is clumsy. It's all practice."

The trail opened onto the north edge of Heron's Cove like a secret in a whisper. The cove's water lay black-green, ironed flat by fog and tide. On the far side, the western bulkhead made a low dark line. A stained fish house squatted at the back of a crushed-shell lot; a cinderblock gear shed hunkered under a pepper tree. A narrow catwalk ran from the fish house to a T-dock where a jon boat bumped a piling with small, impatient thumps—the sound of somebody who needed to be somewhere yesterday.

"Positions," Anya said.

Silas ghosted away toward the rental skiff below the bluff, his shoulders one piece with his oar. Out at the mouth, somewhere you could not see but could feel, Polaris's handler thrummed the water with a patient, heavy presence.

"Carter," Anya said, tapping the warrant. "Front door, knock, announce. Alvarez, you're with him. Keahi, you've got the shed and the catwalk. I'll float between points. Mark and Sarah—we do not break the bubble. You document. You do not touch. Paws stays with Sarah on a six-foot line. If he alerts, you call it. Got it?"

"Got it," Sarah said. Paws' tail tapped once against her shin like a signature.

They crossed the shell lot. At the door of the fish house, Carter banged with the heel of his hand, then lifted his voice to fill the space without scaring the wildlife out of its skin. "Rangers! Sheriff's Office! We have a lawful warrant to enter and search this structure. Announce yourself and open the door!"

Silence took the first sentence and kept it. On the second, somewhere low and interior, something changed its note—a generator hum moving a half-step. Carter gave the required count, then stepped aside. Alvarez's ram hit the latch with a sound like punctuation. The door came in with insulted speed.

Bleach, diesel, a sweet chemical note used to clean sins—like a hospital and a body shop had decided to elope. The room was long, low, concrete-floored, lit by two fluorescents that flickered with intent. Metal tables with fish-scale patinas, stainless sinks that had seen more than fish, a walk-in cooler that wheezed. In the back, a wall of pegboard bristled with lines and hooks inside a gifted teenager's concept of order.

Carter moved center, marker of control. "Clear left," Alvarez called. "Clear right," Keahi echoed from the door of the cooler. No people. Lots of things pretending they were normal.

Paws didn't try to lead. He was trained badly—in love and caution—and well—in the grammar of Sarah's voice—and he heeled until she said his name like a question. "Okay, Paws—look."

He went forward like the world had opened, nose low, path curved, tail writing small paragraphs. He passed the sinks without interest, the cooler with a snort, the pegboard with disdain. At the back wall, where a drain gurgled under the concrete like a throat clearing, he stopped hard and cut his head sideways at a pipe that ran through the cinder block and disappeared toward the bulkhead. He inhaled, coughed, and sneezed twice—the stink of something familiar and wrong. Then he backed up, sat, and looked at Sarah with the patient urgency of someone who has told you twice and expects you to be smart.

"Alert on the effluent," Sarah said, pulse clocking faster. "Same chemical note as last night."

Anya's face went flat. "Photograph everything. Keahi, swing to the shed. If this dump line is active, I want the pump offline now."

Keahi ghosted out. His radio clicked once, then: "Shed is secured. Padlock's cheap. Going in." A beat. "Pump here. Rigged to push from two barrels. Timer on the plug. Somebody loves automation. Killing power."

"Do not pull anything until Fire says we can breathe it," Anya said.

"Copy. I'm breathing in small, disappointed sips."

Sarah worked the camera, angles and scale, footprints in the dust (none), scuffs on the concrete (one, heel-drag), the drain (wet, glistening iridescent), the pipe (PVC, clamped with lazy arrogance). Mark moved behind her writing time stamps, making the kind of notes a defense attorney can chew on and find nothing but paper.

Carter stood by the walk-in cooler and let his hands unfist one knuckle at a time. "Slow water," he said quietly, looking at the drain.

"Donna's whisper," Anya said back, equally low. "They pump on the slack, tuck it under the cove when nobody's watching, and let the incoming tide do the distribution."

"Like a dry cleaner for the conscience," Carter muttered. He turned, scanning, a habit gone bone-deep. "Where's their *right now*?"

The radio answered, Cam's voice sleeping with its eyes open. "Movement," he said. "Small heat signature just left the T-dock. One person. Heading for the jon boat. The boat's outboard is sulking but willing. I've got two bigger heat ghosts tucked under the western bulkhead, low and static. Those are your cold spot from last night—still there, still wrong."

"Silas?" Anya said.

"I'm in the throat," Silas replied. "Fog's a soft glove. If your rabbit runs, I've got a net."

"Keahi," Anya snapped, "out the south door, take the catwalk. If he leaves the dock, you stop being polite."

"On it."

They stepped back into the air—the cove breath colder, the fog thickening like milk poured slow. The catwalk flexed under Keahi's weight as he loped, controlled and quiet, toward the T. The shadow at the jon boat flickered and slipped—a man in a baseball cap and a jacket that thought it was black. He yanked the starter cord; the motor coughed. He yanked again; it caught with a small furious snarl.

"Sir!" Keahi bellowed, acceleration in his legs now, no point in whispering. "Sheriff's Office! Cut the engine!"

The man turned once, saw what the world was made of, and goosed it. The jon boat swung out and tried to aim for the narrow of the cove throat, engine screaming.

Silas didn't run. He stood up in the skiff and threw a line with the kind of care that looks like laziness until you see the loop bite a piling twenty feet away like it was waiting to be held. He took the slack and let the skiff drift, then hummed a noise in his chest that sounded like boats, and the jon boat hit his line as if it had decided to be reasonable. The shock jerked the man sideways and tried to take his feet; he saved himself by accident and landed on the bench with teeth clacked and hands blank. Keahi hit the bow like a linebacker and killed the prop with a twist. The night took a breath.

"Hands," Keahi said, out of breath and still polite. "There you go. On your knees. Here's the part where we talk about your choices."

On the lot, Paws' ears went flat sideways and then forward again. He pivoted and gave the cinderblock shed a look like a question with teeth in it.

Sarah caught it. "One more," she said.

They found the shed as Keahi had left it: padlock cut, door hanging. Inside, two fifty-gallon drums on a pallet, a pump unit welded to a bracket with a timer plug snake-bit into a cheap strip. The smell—sweet, synthetic, a lab in a room that shouldn't have algorithms—caught in the nose and stayed there like guilt.

"Do not breathe deep," Anya said. "Alvarez—photo, photo, photo. Mark, note the timer settings. Sarah—get me the serial on that pump. Keahi, once Fire clears, we're bagging the plug and the timer and our new drums."

The timer had three programs set: **23:05, 01:10, 04:25.** Each for seventy seconds. Enough to burp poison into the cove and walk away with hands clean.

"Whoever set this was punctual," Mark said.

"They'll be early to prison," Carter replied, and for once the bitter humor hit his own ear wrong.

The radio crackled with Morales' voice from the south access road. "Gray Tacoma with a missing magnet frame is creeping down Old Pier Road like it forgot something," she said, dry as sand. "If he remembers too much, I'm going to help him forget."

"Hold the road," Carter said. "If he blinks wrong, make him write it down."

"He's already blinking wrong," Morales said, pleased. "He just doesn't know it yet."

Inside the fish house, Paws reoriented. He ignored the drums now—filed—and went past the sinks, past the cooler, to the back corner where the pegboard ended and the wall began. He exhaled, pressed his nose to what looked like a seam in the drywall that shouldn't have been a seam, and then looked back at Sarah, eyes deeper, urgent and careful.

"Hidden," Sarah said, heart picking up. "He's got a cavity here."

Anya was at her shoulder with a light and a lawyer's memory of warrants. "Wall void," she said. "Our paper covers fixtures and built-ins. It covers hidden compartments. We do this slow. Alvarez, I want a flexible scope. If it's a rat hole, we make a friend. If it's cash, we call Carter and we pray it's sequential."

Alvarez slid the bore-scope in at the seam, the screen blooming into shadow, then into the ribbed belly of a space—plywood, smooth, too clean for vermin. He panned. Plastic. The edge of a hard case. A zipper pull catching the light.

"Santa," Alvarez said softly. "You got here early."

"Documented," Anya said. "Carter—hidden compartment, back wall of fish house. Potential evidence container inside. We're going to pop the face if the fasteners are basic."

"Do it," Carter said. "If it's live paperwork, it's getting cold out there."

They pulled the panel with the care of surgeons and thieves. It fought like a thing that knew it didn't belong. The screws were strip-headed and angry. The panel detached with a reluctant sigh. Inside, two waterproof duffels, a pelican-style hard case, and a stack of thick, sealed envelopes strapped with rubber bands—cash bundles the color of bad decisions.

Carter stood there for a second, eyebrows winged. "Photograph. Count what we can see. Do not cut those bands. Someone's going to love those latent prints."

Anya gestured Sarah forward. Red light, scale, hands gloved and out of frame. The camera ate everything.

"Mark," Anya said, "I want a label on that cavity lip—time, date, who opened. I want it to read like a eulogy."

Keahi ducked in, damp from the catwalk, the jon boat's fugitive cuffed and coughing in county's back seat outside. He saw the money and didn't smile. "Our boy says his name is Kaleb and his job description is 'just transport.' He also says he's never heard of Donna Vale and he's never seen a drum in his life. He's willing to sell his mother for a promise and a soda."

"He can tell the soda to his public defender," Carter said. "We'll pour him a tall one if his brain learns to use verbs."

Anya popped the Pelican case latches with two fingers like she didn't trust any plastic that smiled that easy. Inside, under foam cut like a brief's outline, lay a folder of not paper but laminated prints—satellite grabs and LIDAR charts of the coast annotated by a hand that liked specifics. Red circles at the turtle nesting sites, blue lines marking drift predictions at varying wind speeds, black Xs at the "slow water" dead zones. Across the bottom of one, a note: HERON'S:

THROW UNDER BULKHEAD, WEST SIDE, -1.2 to +0.8 TIDE. DO NOT MIX BEFORE 2300.

Anya looked at Sarah with a face that held fury very still. "They didn't just know the beach," she said. "They knew the ocean."

"Maps," Sarah said, throat tight. "We've got them. We've got the plan."

"Photo," Carter said, voice tin, something behind his eyes going quiet. "Then bag. Then call the DA and tell her we're bringing her Sunday reading."

Cam's voice slipped in again, amused despite fog and felony. "While you were opening early Christmas, I went and looked at that heat puddle, because nobody told me not to loudly enough. We've got two cold lockers bolted to the underside of the bulkhead, each with chain and thrift-store anchors. Your pump line kisses the water six feet away. Those boxes are giving me the kind of thermal that says sealed and smug."

"Do not touch," Anya snapped reflexively, then moderated. "Silas—we're going to need your back and

Fire's booms. We'll secure the area and come at those lockers like we've met physics."

"Physics is a polite neighbor if you bake them something," Silas said. "I'll bring bread."

County Fire humped booms down the trail like fat orange snakes. Tac Fire's lieutenant—a woman with forearms like a rower and a voice that made men nod—laid out absorbent pads and spill socks with the reverence of an altar. "You tell me when," she said to Anya. "We'll build you a halo."

"Do it," Anya said.

They circled the bulkhead outflow, laid booms on black water, the orange arcs catching fog and turning it to ugly poetry. Silas slid into the cove in the skiff with a hook and a sling, patient as a heron. At the pilings, he feathered the oar, let the skiff's nose kiss wood, and leaned down like he was telling secrets to the tide. His hook found the chain by the tell-tale scrape scars. He gave it a lover's tug and felt resistance like a stubborn mule.

"Got your fridge," he said. "She doesn't want to come up. She will."

He looped the sling, signaled ready. On the catwalk, Keahi and Alvarez took the line, leaned, and put a slow, enormous human will into it. The chain shrugged; the locker's corner showed itself through the water—a steel-gray rectangle with blue paint at one end and a handprint smeared where someone had tried to hold their guilt steady.

"Up slow," Anya said. "Everybody breathe smaller."

They brought the box to the surface. Fog slicked off it like sweat. Fire set absorbent around it like a wreath. Anya crouched. The padlock was budget-grade. She looked at Carter.

"Paper?"

"Paper," he said, tapping the warrant. "Open."

Alvarez cut the lock. The lid lifted slow, the rubber gasket making a small, indecent sound. Inside, four plastic jerricans with screw tops. Two were half empty.

One slopped a viscous, rainbow-thick liquid. The fourth was unlabeled and still sealed. A faint haze reached up and stung Sarah's eyes.

"Stop," Tac Fire said sharply. "Masks on. If you're not instrumented, you're out."

Paws stood, hackles trying to do two things at once—rise and not. Sarah put a hand on his collar and murmured nothing words into his ear. He licked his nose, sneezed, and decided to sit on his own tail, as if anchoring himself to the planet.

Tac Fire's meter burped and blinked. "Not explosive," the lieutenant said. "Bad for lungs and turtles. We're good to bag and tag if you don't breathe like it's a yoga class."

"Swabs," Anya said, and Sarah felt the practical calm settle her like a hand between her shoulder blades. She labeled vials with a Sharpie that sang on the tape and then swabbed: gasket, lid, handle, the outside of the jerrican, the inside lip where a sloppy pourer had left his name in chemistry. Mark wrote the numbers and the time and the weather and the witnesses. Alvarez photographed the hell out of it. Boring built its nest inside crisis and made itself at home.

Cam coughed into the radio theatrically. "Second fridge, same as the first. Chain's pouting. Want me to hum at it again?"

"Do it," Anya said, then into county air: "Morales, status?"

Morales replied with delight in it. "Our gray Tacoma's driver had a little argument with the concept of registration," she said. "He also has a bed full of empty totes and a floor full of fish scale. His story is that he's lost. His eyes say he's found."

"Hold him," Carter said. "No search beyond what your warrant permits—we'll roll the paper down to you after we finish kissing refrigerators."

"Copy. He already hates me. Today is rich."

Up at the fish house, the hidden duffels yielded to tags with as much protest as fabric can make. The cash got counted visually, not touched. The envelopes wore bank stamps from three different counties, which meant three different stories or one careful one. The Pelican's maps went into a clean folder that felt heavier than paper should.

On the desk next to the wall void, a phone vibrated where someone had tried to leave it pretending to be a wrench. The screen blinked one message into a locked notification: GULLWING 02: HOLD. LAWYER COMPROMISED. DROP SITE MOVED. The number showed as nothing but a ghost.

Carter stared. "Gullwing," he said, like the word tasted like pretension. "That's not a boat. That's a habit."

"Photograph," Anya said. "Then bag, then Faraday sleeve. We don't wake it up until a judge gives us a toothbrush for its teeth."

"Cam," Sarah said, because she couldn't help the thought that hopped like a fish, "if they moved the drop site—"

"—they still have to run the Tongue or the back channel," Cam finished. "And fog or no fog, Polaris is the big thing on the water that everything else has to pretend not to notice. We'll bump any hull that looks like a bad idea."

Paws tugged once—soft, a thread on Sarah's wrist. She followed his look, thinking he'd found another seam, but his stare had gone farther, through the door, across the lot, toward the boathouse tucked in the crook where scrub swallowed it. It sat low, wood gone gray, padlock newer than its neighbors. It meant to look like it had always been closed.

"Anya," Sarah said, pulse ticked up again, "him."

Anya turned, then checked the last page of the paper stack, the tertiary warrant signed on three hours' sleep by a judge with a tight pen. "Boathouse is covered on probable from last night's aerial," she said. "We do it, but we do it slow. We've already found a pump, a wall, a cooler full of wrong. They'll have wired a surprise for dessert."

The boathouse door wore a padlock that tried to look cheap. Alvarez cut it without drama. "Knock, announce," Carter said, because you say the script even when the theatre is empty. "Rangers. Sheriff's Office. Lawful warrant."

Silas, on the catwalk, watched water like a farmhand watches weather. The fog had thinned, the air moving in the cove not through wind but through the tide's slow rotation—a spoon stirring a dark cup.

Anya nodded, and Alvarez swung the door. It opened a third and stopped—something behind it catching and pulsing.

"Trip," Keahi said instantly. He dropped to his belly and slid an eye to the crack like a mechanic listening to a carb. "Monofilament to a hook tied to a can. If you pull, you ring like you're late for church. And"—he smelled it, not saw it—"they spritz you with something you don't invite to the party."

"Cut at the can," Anya said. "Not the line. If they dusted the line, I want it."

Keahi clipped, Alvarez bagged, Mark wrote, Sarah's camera made the small warmth of work. They opened the door the rest of the way with a broom handle like a nervous uncle.

Inside, a small boat slept—twenty-three feet, aluminum-sided, low center console, the kind that minds its business and carries too much weight. It didn't have a name on the hull. It *did* have a smear on the gunwale like a careless thumb—dark, gummy, rainbow in the red light.

"Photograph," Anya said. "Do not touch that yet. I want a first swab on that smear and a second after we wipe it and a third on the wipe."

Sarah worked the swabs. The chemical note climbed her sinuses and rang a bell—last night's drums, the effluent pipe. Paws sneezed, then forced himself to be bored because sometimes the bravest thing you can be is nothing at all.

"Check the deck," Carter said, voice more grindstone than throat now. "You don't run poison and money out of a fish house without a place to hide both and go home thinking you'll have soup."

They moved around the console. It was clean—too clean. The screw heads on one section of deck looked newer than the rest. Alvarez crouched, rapped the panel. It thudded like a lie. He put the Phillips in and backed the fasteners in a quick cross, brilliant with habit. The panel lifted, not enough to do anything with, just enough to let a smell out—money, oil, something animal that had been there and decided not to admit it.

Anya held the warrant up out of sheer superstition and said, "Open," like she was speaking to a courtroom. Alvarez got his fingers under and raised. Inside lay waterproof bags—two gray, one olive, one black—stacked compact like the thought of regret. A corner of a Pelican case showed underneath like the hard edge of a secret. A folded tarp wrapped something that didn't make a shape your brain wanted to name.

"No one touch," Anya said. "Photograph every inch. If a gnat farts, I want it in focus."

Sarah did, breath small, heart big. Mark wrote dates like he was chiseling. Carter stood like he'd been built to be steady in moments when somebody else would pace. Keahi and Alvarez both had their edges turned outward, making a channel for whatever the day was about to pour.

"Cam," Carter said into the radio, not taking his eyes off the boat, "be advised—primary boat seized. Hidden hold present and photographed. We're going to secure it here and tow it up to the lot for forensics. If you see a cousin of this hull moving, you tell me before it thinks it's thought."

"Roger," Cam said. "Fog's lifting its skirt. I can see your ears again."

Tac Fire's lieutenant leaned into the boathouse doorway, mask slung at her neck now, gases cooperative. "You want me to put a monitor in here while you play with your new toy?"

"Please," Anya said. "If anything in that hold hisses, I want to know before my eyebrows do."

While the monitor chirped steady and harmless, Sarah made one more pass with her lens and caught what her eye had slid past: on the underside of the deck panel, in trailer-marker scrawl, the numbers 184 inked three times. She took the photo, said the number aloud without meaning to.

"Good catch," Carter said. "We've got '184' on the blue bundle last night. We've got it on a note in Vale's case. That makes it a Rosetta stone or somebody's locker combination. Either way, it's a tie."

"Bag the panel separate," Anya said. "Prints, DNA, universe."

Outside, the dawn was coming on enough to be called morning. The fog lifted in columns like ghosts shucking sheets. The cove's water took color. The bulkhead looked like what it was—a wooden faith holding dirt back from a greedy sea.

The second locker came up foul and heavy. Inside, not jerricans but two sealed bins, smaller, with stainless mesh baskets nested inside each. In one, a handful of cracked turtle eggshells—the edges stained with the rainbow sheen of the same polite poison. In the other, a tangle of nylon net cut short, smelling of rot and solvent. The kind of tools you bring to a nursery if you are the wrong kind of person.

Sarah swallowed a word she didn't want on tape and took the photographs that hurt to take. "These are the originals," she said, voice thin. "The stuff that tore up nests five nights ago." The thought landed like a nail. "They kept them. They sink them and pick them up when no one is watching. Trophies or tools. Either way—"

"Cause," Carter said. "Direct. Not abstract. A judge eats this for breakfast, lunch, and a press conference."

"Careful," Anya said softly. "We don't let righteous do our job. We let process do it. Righteous will get its turn."

Silas looked up from the skiff, sun coming into his eyes, fish crow calling from the mangrove. "You can hear the cove say *thank you*," he said. "But you better bring it stew, not soup."

Morales' voice came over the radio, businesslike joy at a low simmer. "South unit to Command. We have our Tacoma driver consenting to nothing and catching his breath loudly. In plain view—bin bags, boot prints in sludge, a stuck-on scale that looks like sturgeon but is not. If your paper gets here, we will open his honesty for him. If not, we'll sit on him until the earth cools."

"Paper is on its way," Carter said. "Anya—"

"—I'll run it down once we secure the sites and chain-of-custody. You," she said to Carter, "sit on my boathouse."

"Gladly."

They worked the last hour like they were being graded by a ghost. The drums came out of the shed in white hazmat bags; the pump came apart the way a lie falls apart when you ask it for its eighth detail. The effluent pipe got capped and taped and tagged. The fish house cooler yielded two labels in its drain with serials that matched a set of invoices in the hard case—shell corporations buying solvents from a warehouse that used to sell paint thinner and now sold deniability.

They walked the boathouse with a vacuum for trace, pulling hairs, fibers, the story you tell when you don't think you're telling any story at all. On the boat's console, under the lip, someone had stuck a cigarette butt like a tiny flag. It had lipstick on it—color expensive, name probably criminal—Vale's mouth or someone else's show of loyalty. They tweezed it and bagged it.

When they finally towed the boat up the lot—Silas steering the skiff slow, Mark and Keahi walking the line, the boat following like a horse that had decided to behave—the fog thinned to lace. The sun shot loose of the low cloud and threw rose and gold across the cove, turning the boathouse's gray back into silver.

On the bluff, the gate had gotten busy. People with coffee stood shaped by concern. Fishermen with faces like weather had their arms crossed. Mrs. Gable had turned the tailgate into a preschool for hope. Leo held up a hand-lettered sign that read QUIET FOR TURTLES and shushed a gull like it was a cousin.

Sophie saw the boat come up and didn't move forward because rules had been explained and she was old enough now to understand that breaking them is how you hurt the people you love. But she stood taller and put her hands on the fence and watched with a face you file away so you can recognize it later when she has keys and a job and a whole other coastline in her head.

Paws let out one breath, then two, slow, a release valve on a machine that had done its job and was allowed to be an animal again. Sarah scratched the base of his ear, grateful enough to be cruel.

Cam came up the path in a rumor of coffee and salt, cap back on his head, grin reduced from full to civilized. "You left me the fun part," he said, nodding at the boat. "I like you best when you leave me toys."

"Don't touch my toys," Anya said. "You can look at my toys. You can tell my toys a story. You may not touch them."

"Story it is," Cam said. He looked at the lockers on their absorbent beds, the drums in their bags, the boat with its hidden stomach, the stack of mapped intelligence in its labeled box. He sobered like a tide going out. "You cooked them," he said quietly. "You actually cooked them."

"We set a table," Carter replied. "Jury eats."

The tall woman's name traveled up the bluff on someone's phone, on someone's cousin's text: out on bail, high-and-mighty, a whisper that you can buy gravity if you know the number. Carter heard it in the shape of his own jaw setting. He looked at the boat and then at the cove and then at Sophie's sign rocked by a small hand.

"Paper," Anya said to him, reading his face the way she read ocean. "Go get my paper to Morales. Tell the DA to get out of bed in something that doesn't look like she slept in her car."

"I'll go," Carter said, fatigue making the decision before his feet did. He looked at Sarah. "You ride with me. You have eyes. You saw the timer. You saw the maps. If anyone asks me what we saw, I want a second witness whose memory is a lens."

Sarah glanced at Paws. The dog looked back and then to Sophie and then to the boat and then to the cove. He thumped his tail once, as if to say, *I'll lend you out. I'll stay here. Everyone gets what they're good at.*

"I'll stay with him," Sophie said from the fence, as if the dog had spoken. "He understands boring. I can do boring."

"You're why boring wins," Carter said, and meant it.

They loaded boxes like altar gifts into the back of the truck. The Pelican went in. The duffels, still sealed, went in. The panel with 184 went in. The phone in its silver bag. The folders in their clean sleeves. Mark checked every number on every piece of tape out loud.

Anya put a signature next to each with a pen that left a groove. Chain-of-custody looked like a genealogy.

Morales' voice came on the radio one last time, a punctuation mark. "South to Command," she said. "Our Tacoma driver has remembered his lawyer's number. He says a tall woman with red lipstick told him nothing ever sticks in this county. I told him asphalt does and so will this. He would like to see my supervisor. I told him he's looking at her."

Carter smiled with half his mouth at nothing and everything. "On my way with the paper," he said. He looked at Anya. "Watch my boat."

"It's not your boat," Anya said.

"It's ours," he corrected.

Silas leaned on the skiff's gunwale and watched the cove change color by color like a story being retold with better adjectives. "You know what slow water does," he said to nobody and everybody. "It looks still. It keeps secrets. But it holds things on the bottom until somebody puts a hook in right. You put a hook in."

Anya looked at the lockers, the drums, the boat, the faces at the fence, the dog lying with his paws crossed like patience dressed as fur. "We put a hook in," she said, and let herself be tired for one breath, then put it down.

They towed the boat to the main beach because light and space make evidence behave. Tac Fire rode behind with their halo, booms ready in case anything decided to kiss the sand that shouldn't. County's truck with the drums in their white shrouds followed like a hearse for bad ideas. The convoy made a strange small parade through town—fog shedding, people lifting coffee cups, heads turning, some clapping without meaning to when they saw the rangers' jackets and the boat and the dog and the way purpose sits on a group like armor you share.

When they pulled into the beach lot, the east had turned to ordered light. The surf said *you're late but I'll allow it*. The command post got rebuilt in the time it takes a practiced hand to tear and tape. Forensics set up their trays. The DA arrived with hair that said she'd slept three hours and a jacket that said she could cut a throat with precedent. She shook Anya's hand like both of them knew how to take a compliment and not show their teeth.

"You gave me a holiday," the DA said, nodding at the stack of paper and plastic. "I brought you a judge who likes turtles and hates sloppy." She looked at the boat's hold, at the number 184 on the deck panel. "We'll talk about numerology later."

"Talk about conspiracy first," Carter said, setting the box with the Pelican on the table like a brick in a foundation. "We have maps of nesting sites and currents. We have a pump on a timer. We have drums with a chemical that matches the sheen on those bins. We have a phone that thinks it's smarter than it is. We have a Tacoma that thinks it's a priest confessional. And we have a bar out there that would like to testify."

The DA's mouth did the thing that can be smile or baring. "Chain-of-custody is my bedtime story," she said. "Tell me the one where nothing gets thrown out."

Mark started at the beginning and told it all: five-oh-six first knock, five-oh-nine door breach, five-eleven wall cavity found by canine alert, five-fifteen panel removed, five-eighteen Pelican case inventoried, five-twenty-two phone located, five-thirty pump disabled at the shed, five-forty-three locker one raised, five-fifty-seven locker two raised, six-ten boathouse entry, six-thirteen deck panel removed, six-fifteen hold photographed, six-eighteen seal of hold not disturbed, six-twenty-five tow began, seven-oh-one arrival beach lot. He didn't look up while he said it. He didn't need to. He knew the faces the times made.

"Good," the DA said. "You all get a gold star and maybe sleep in two days. Carter—go back to Morales. Hold your Tacoma. We've got paper for it. I want to see if our friend's floor mats can tell me when they last confessed."

Carter went. Anya turned to the boat and rolled her shoulders like you do when a big job starts where a bigger one ends. She looked at Sarah and then at Paws. "You good?" she asked the dog like he had a badge.

He thumped his tail and sighed, and that was enough.

"Alright," Anya said to the day. "Let's open our present."

They lifted the deck panel they'd already photographed. The hold smelled like plastic and salt and a chemical that made your tongue remember you shouldn't. Inside, the duffels sat like rocks.

Anya cut the strap of the **first** and opened with the care you give a snake that might be asleep. Cash. Stacks of it. Strapped with bank bands. Numbers printed along the sides like they meant something organized.

The **second** bag: maps again, this time hand-sketched additions to the laminated prints, routes drawn with arrows that curved around the Tongue like a lover's finger.

The **third** bag: notebooks, spiral-bound, the covers cheap, the contents not—columns of dates, times, initials.

The **last**: equipment—night vision monocular, two radios, a small handheld spectrometer with a fingerprint smudge on its screen.

Paws' tail ticked twice, not because he cared about money, but because the room had agreed with his nose. He laid his head on his paws and went still—guarding. He didn't know about slow water as a concept. He knew about bad smell and good people and the worked-out work of staying.

Sarah shot it all and felt something in her chest unwind that had been coiled for too long. The oily smear on the gunwale got its comparative swab; the drums got their sample slips; the lockers' baskets got counted like eggs in reverse. Boring had built a cathedral and set out candles.

Out past the bar, the fog had burned to tatters, and Polaris sat on the horizon like a promise written in steel. Gulls stitched the sky. In the shallows, a small school of finger mullet flashed once, then vanished into the idea of a better day.

Silas drifted a little away from the group, took his cap off, and rubbed the back of his neck with a hand that knew ropes. He looked at the dog, then the kid with the sign, then the sea that would outlast all of them. "Slow water holds," he said, voice for himself. "But it gives back if you ask right."

Anya heard him and didn't turn. "We asked," she said. "We didn't beg. That's the difference."

By eight-thirty, the beach had a different kind of crowd. People who had followed the sirens now followed the smell of something happening. The story would go out in concentric circles—text threads, local feeds, a picture of a Doodle dog in front of a boat with a deck open and a ranger with a gloved hand reaching for a notebook. There would be anger; there would be relief; there would be the other thing no one names because superstition hates ambition: momentum.

Somebody brought pastries because this is how you love people who are holding your world together. Somebody else set a coffee urn down with a clank because this is how you weaponize kindness. Mrs. Gable kept the KIDS' CORNER humming like a small factory of future.

And through it all, under it and around it, Paws watched, cataloged, breathed, and was. He would be the first to notice if anything went wrong. He would be the first to relax when everything went right. He would know when slow water stopped being a threat and went back to being part of the place he loved.

Carter called at 09:12, voice thinner with the long morning.

"Morales' Tacoma consented after paper," he said. "Floor mats match your effluent. Bed had a false side—bolts from the inside. Inside that—spools of monofilament pre-strung with treble hooks. Same style as your trail. Also a printed list: 'S—Sunset Nests, H—Heron's, BB—Back Bay.' Initials match your notebook times. We have us a ledger."

"Bring it," the DA said, already reaching for a pen to sign for things she had wanted for two months.

Cam added, because he cannot not: "And if you wanted a bow on this, some brain genius with a drone just tried to fly over your lot to get sweet content. I whispered to his signal with Polaris's toys, and his drone decided to go have a nap. He is about to learn about FAA rules from a man who speaks in bullet points."

"Do not tase the influencer," Anya said, not because she feared Cam would but because she enjoyed telling him not to do things he already knew not to do.

"I will not. I will use words like a civilized fish," Cam said. "Polaris out."

At 10:03, when the paperwork had acquired so many signatures that it looked like a petition, the tide reached its turn and paused—the whole ocean holding its breath at Heron's Cove. For a heartbeat the water went mirror. In that moment, Sarah saw their faces doubled—an upside-down world that looked steadier than the right way up. She thought of last night's warning, of the text typed and never sent—*Tides are predictable*—and felt the old fear pass a hand over her scalp and go. Its fingers were cold. Its palm was warm. It left her with the shape of the day impressed under her skin.

Sophie stepped close to Paws and put her hand on his neck. "Slow water's not scary anymore," she whispered, like you whisper to a dog so the world can hear. "It's just a place where we have to be smart."

Paws exhaled and leaned into her, and the beach got on with the business of making heroes out of boring people and putting villains in the places where the air is worse and the coffee never quite hot enough.

By the time the tide paused at slack, the cove held their reflections as if weighing them. The next hours would be the cold work—tweezers and tape, spectrums and serials, signatures stacked until truth had a paper spine.

For now the skiff rocked once and went still, the seized boat lay open like a gutted lie, and the orange booms wrote a bright parenthesis around everything they refused to lose. Paws leaned against Sophie's shin.

Slow water had kept its secrets a long time; it hadn't kept them today. And when the tide turned, they were ready to follow it.

Chapter 9
CONFRONTATION AND CAPTURE

The pre-dawn air lay heavy and unmoving over Sunset Beach, a hush so complete it made every breath feel borrowed. The white noise of surf was a slow pulse in the dark, steady enough to hide a human heartbeat, not enough to mask the hum of a careful engine.

From their crawl of dune grass above Heron's Cove, Mark and Sophie Reynolds lay flat, binoculars and camera lenses rimed with salt. Between them, Paws kept his chin on the sand, golden coat darkened with fog, ears forward and nose at work. The wind was a thin thread off the water—just enough to bring the acrid tang the family now recognized: solvent, oil, a chemical note that didn't belong to tide or marsh.

Sophie felt the dog's chest vibrate before she heard it—the low, contained hum he'd been trained to give instead of a bark. Mark's hand found the thick ruff at Paws's neck and stilled. On the black water, a low silhouette slid toward the cove: narrow beam, cutback transom, matte hull that swallowed moonlight. Two shadows stood in the cockpit. The boat's engine idled barely above a whisper.

"Reynolds to base," Mark murmured into the throat mic, eyes never leaving the boat. "Vessel inbound Heron's Cove. Dark hull, low profile, two aboard. Paws alerts on chemical scent."

Miles offshore in the camouflaged observation post, Ranger David Hayes leaned closer to his console. He could hear the sea in the open mics, the hush of wind through grass, the soft static of his own breath. "Copy, Reynolds. Coast Guard is standing off the point. All units hold position until infraction is observed."

On another channel, a fisherman's voice came quick and quiet. "Silas here. Ranger, we've got a second contact peeling north by the oyster beds—a skiff. Running dark, hugging the marsh. Smaller, two souls aboard. Do you want us to shadow?"

Hayes weighed it, eyes flicking to the clock. They'd rehearsed this, but rehearsals never sweat of their own accord. "Negative, Silas. Maintain visual only. If they beach, mark it and call it. Primary target remains Heron's Cove."

"Roger that. We'll keep our lanterns asleep," Silas said, and the line went soft.

In the cove, the smugglers cut throttle. The little boat ghosted into the pale slice of beach between mangrove roots. One man jumped to the sand and caught a painter; the other heaved a canister down into waiting arms. A second canister followed. The hiss of wet rope, muted curses, a hissed "Hurry."

Paws gave another of those contained thrum-sounds, his body a coiled spring. Sophie, breath fogging the edge of her viewfinder, tracked the men as they shouldered into the shade of overhang and brush.

"They're unloading," Mark whispered. "Two metal canisters to shore. Both wearing deck gloves. I've got photos."

Hayes's voice in his ear stayed low and steady. "Copy, Reynolds. That's our probable cause. All units, phase one. Sharma, take your team to the east approach and stand by. Coast Guard, you are go for seaward intercept when they push off."

"Coast Guard copies," came a woman's clipped reply. "Cutter Argent moving to position."

In the hush that follows a greenlight, time stretches oddly. The men in the cove worked with a practiced urgency, every movement built for muscle memory and speed. The one in the boat glanced toward the mouth of the cove twice, nerves buzzing in the tiny motions of his hands. Then his head snapped up.

He heard something.

The man on the sand froze, half-hidden by mangrove shade. For a beat, only gulls and surf. Then a sound—a deep, distant thrum—bloomed and died as the Coast Guard's engines spooled briefly and fell. A whisper on the water. A warning on a smuggler's skin.

"Go," the man hissed, already scrambling. Canisters were abandoned where they had been set. The boat's engine jumped from idle to throatier growl, bow swinging for open water. The man on the beach ran shin-deep and hauled himself over the gunwale in a spray of phosphorescence.

"Now," Hayes said, not loud, not soft; a word that turned watchers into a net.

Searchlights ignited over the cove like a sunrise in fast-forward, spearing down the throat of the channel as the Argent slid past the point. The little boat did what little boats do—it tried to be smaller. It threw spray. It went for the one escape that wasn't a straight line: a tight, shallow channel of rock and sandbars locals called Serpent's Tongue. It was a dangerous cut even at mid-tide. At a falling tide, it was a dare.

Silas's voice hit the net again, tight with urgency. "Ranger, they're aiming for the Tongue. The ledges there eat props for breakfast. Tide's dropping—tell the cutter to mind her draft."

Hayes relayed, already hearing the Coast Guard commander answer calm and professional: "Copy, local conditions noted. We have shallow-water sonar hot and a drone overhead. We'll pressure without grounding."

Paws whined once, torn between the bright line of boats and the dark shapes left on the sand. Sophie squeezed his collar. "Stay," she whispered, eyes never leaving the men's abandoned work.

"Canisters first," Mark said. "Document position. Down to the waterline before tide smudges it." He slid down the dune face, boots soft on the face of sand. Sophie followed, camera strapped and clicking in short deliberate bursts. Paws came last, doing what Paws did best: nose down, mind sharp, attention on the tiny things humans forget to watch.

The canisters were stainless, round-shouldered, valves taped, each with a residue smear that stained the sand an ugly sheen. The scent up close was worse—sweet-metallic, wrong. Mark snapped quick photos, then backed his phone away from the potential hazard and keyed the radio. "Two canisters located. We're marking and holding. Possible additional item on site."

"Additional item?" Hayes asked.

"There." Sophie pointed to a dark shape half-buried near the high-tide wrack. Not a shell, not seaweed: a small waterproof satchel, the kind kayakers used when they cared more about what was inside than the bag itself. Someone had dropped it in a hurry.

Mark set a clean evidence sack down, tugged nitrile gloves from his pocket, and eased the satchel out with two fingers. Weighty. When he unzipped it he found rolled maps rubber-banded into tight scrolls, a small metal thumb drive in a crush-proof sleeve, and a notebook that had seen rain and hard hands. Page edges curled, ink blurred, but readable. Numbers, coordinates, hand-drawn channel notations with fishhooks and skulls marking hazards. On the inside flap, an embossed logo for an industrial waste contractor surfaced in dull light.

Sophie leaned in, camera angled. "I know that logo," she said, voice tight. "From the articles Mom saved—about that company that 'lost' a shipment of solvents up the coast last year."

Before Mark could answer, Paws left the tidy circle of their find and nosed toward a mess of driftwood and storm-thrown sea oats. His tail stiffened. He pawed lightly, then looked back at Mark, eyes bright and waiting.

"What do you smell?" Mark said, forcing calm into his tone. He eased closer and gently pulled aside the top layer of bleached sticks. A small canvas bag lay in a shallow scrape in the sand, edges dark with damp. He lifted it into the sodium glow of Sophie's headlamp and unknotted the thong. Inside: smaller snap-top vials with a viscous, dark liquid, a laminated card printed with chemical formulas and a phone number, and—wedged into a corner—an envelope in a zip bag.

Handwritten on the envelope in a narrow, slanted hand: If you are a ranger and not one of them, look at Beacon Reclamation's invoices—ask for "Inez." We are not all dirty. Burn this.

Mark felt a small, electric prick walk his spine. He lifted the card and turned it over. Same contractor logo. The back had been scuffed by sand, but someone had pressed a thumb there hard enough to leave a crescent of grit.

"Whistleblower?" Sophie asked, barely above a breath.

"Maybe," Mark said, mind clicking through what that meant. "Maybe someone inside trying to talk without getting killed for it."

A cracked branch popped behind them.

Paws swiveled first—always first—and his chest rumbled into a sound that could make a smart person stop. A figure rose from the dark notch where dune met scrub: lean, hooded, the kind of stillness that comes with predatory patience. A lookout. He'd been there the whole time.

"Back away," the man said. His voice was soft and flat, an unthreatening tone that somehow felt more dangerous than a bark. In one hand, something glinted. Not a gun—too slim. A fillet knife. The blade held easy and low.

Sophie froze. Mark didn't, because parents never do when their children stop breathing. He moved enough to block her with his body. "We're not heroes," he said, hands open, all truth. "You should go before the place is full of uniformed people who like bracelets."

"You picked the wrong night to sightsee," the man said, and stepped closer.

Paws did not move toward the knife. He moved so the knife would have to come through him to reach Sophie. The sound he made now was different—less trained, more ancient. It stopped the man mid-step. In that half-second of pause, Sophie did something she didn't plan to do but had practiced her whole life without knowing it: she brought the camera to her eye and hit the flash full in his face.

The burst of light carved the world into negative and blind spots. The man flinched and brought one hand up. That was all Paws needed. The dog pushed forward and hit the man at the thigh, not to bite, but to change balance. The knife hand swung; the point pricked Paws's shoulder and scored fur and skin, a hot line that made Sophie's stomach drop. Mark lunged, shoulder-first, and the three of them went to sand in a tumble where grass met tide debris.

"Police!" Officer Anya Sharma's voice cut the dark like a line through canvas. "Drop it! Hands!"

Sharma and Ranger Sarah Jenkins came in from the flank, boots sure on the unstable sand. A third ranger ghosted from the other side. The man's survival instinct asserted itself: he ditched the knife and went loose, palms out, face composed to neutral. Zip ties bit his wrists. Sharma kicked the knife back, eyes never leaving the captive.

"You all right?" Sharma asked, breath hard but steady, gaze flicking to Paws, to the thin, dark line on his shoulder.

Sophie's hand found Paws's ear. "He's bleeding," she said, and Paws shook once, dismissing pain the way dogs do. He leaned gently against her knee and breathed like a ship's bellows.

Jenkins knelt, tore open a small field kit, and pressed a gauze pad against the shallow wound. "It's surface," she said. "Ugly, not deep. Good boy." Paws's tail thumped once, restrained and grateful.

Sharma's radio crackled. Static hissed, then the calm Coast Guard voice again: "Suspect vessel entering narrow channel. We are in parallel pursuit with drone feed. Prepare to copy."

Hayes came over the open channel. "All ground units, stand by. Argent, keep it on tape."

What followed came in clipped bursts across the net and later in the official record, but even live it felt like an after-action you could breathe:

USCGC ARGENT — BOARDING LOG (EXCERPT)

0431Z — Visual acquire: 22 ft. go-fast, 2 POB, course 121°, speed 28 kts.

0433Z — Suspects enter Serpent's Tongue; depth drops to 4.8 ft. at mid-channel. Drone overhead; sonar marks shoal at 30 m starboard.

0435Z — Hailing on 16; no response. Suspects increase throttle; wake indicates cavitation.

0436Z — Contact with submerged ledge audible/visible; suspect vessel loses steerage, grounds on rocky shelf. Engines cut.

0437Z — Boarding team launches RHIB; non-compliant posture observed; OC deployed.

0439Z — Both suspects secured in flex cuffs. Scene safe. Commencing evidence preservation and hull inspection. Video and audio rolling.

As the cutter's floodlight held the wrecked go-fast in a clean, hard circle, the men inside coughed and cursed and sagged to their knees. The night gave a heartbeat back to Heron's Cove.

"Primary suspects in custody," Hayes said, his voice like flint finally allowed to cool. "Sharma, good collar on the lookout. Reynolds—you still with me?"

"We're here," Mark said. His gloves were smeared where he'd pressed gauze to Paws. He felt awake in a way caffeine could not create. "We've secured canisters, maps, drive, a laminated card with formulae and the contractor logo—in addition to a note from an apparent insider. Sophie has photos. We've also got evidence of a shallow burial with vials—liquid samples."

"Copy all," Hayes said. "Hold your perimeter. We'll get forensics down."

A small sigh escaped Sophie's lungs then, as if she'd been holding a stone under her ribs. Paws nosed her wrist as if to tell her the same thing Mark was thinking: it was not over, but something had ended.

But the night had one more thread unspooling.

"Ranger," Silas whispered back on the net, voice lowered as if the marsh itself could over hear. "That skiff I mentioned—she shut down on a grassy spit up in the estuary. Lights still dark. I can see two figures hauling a crate into the reeds. If that's a secondary drop we'll lose the tide in twenty. You want eyes closer?"

Hayes looked at his board. Too many pins, not enough hands. "Sharma, do you have two to spare?"

Sharma glanced at Jenkins and then at the glint of Paws's eye. "I have one ranger and a dog and a very motivated parent," she said. "We shadow. We don't engage until I say."

Mark didn't wait for permission—he should have, but some permissions you carry inside you already stamped. "We'll go," he said. "We'll stay on you." Sophie opened her mouth, already forming the argument that would keep her next to Paws, but Sharma beat her to it.

"You're with us, Soph," she said. "You're our camera. You stay a body's length behind me at all times. If I say 'down,' you drop. That's the deal."

Sophie nodded, throat clicking. She slid the camera strap tight across her chest—less a recorder now than a tool.

Jenkins handed Mark a small roll of orange survey flagging tape. "Drop a tab every twenty yards on a branch or grass clump," she said. "If we have to bug out fast, it will get us back through the dark."

They moved off the beach into the black-green of the marsh path, a vein between walls of needlerush and spartina. The smell changed: iodine, old mud, the metallic ghost of washed-up storms. The tide was running out in narrow gutters, water whispering through grass roots like talk you can't quite make out. Paws led, nose low and tail a line. Every third step he paused, lifted his head, tested the air.

"Watch your feet," Sharma warned. "Crab holes. And hooks. Some of these guys set trip lines."

They found the first one five minutes in—a nylon monofilament stretched shin-high between two stakes, dressed with seaweed to make it look like trash. Paws stopped dead and put his paw on the line so gently Sophie could barely see it. Sharma squatted, snapped a photo, and cut the filament with a multi-tool. "That's a hook bank," she said, pointing to the margin where the line disappeared into the grass. "Barbed trebles tied off under the water. Nasty."

"People put that... here?" Sophie whispered, incredulous anger sparking. "Where the birds feed?"

"And where people bleed if they go the wrong way," Sharma said. "Stay light on your feet."

They moved another hundred yards, the marsh opening into a flat of mud that could take a human to the knee if they misstepped. At the edge of a little cove eaten out of the reeds, Paws stiffened and lifted his head. He took two slow breaths and looked left. Mark trusted the dog's nose more than any compass now. He followed the look and saw it: a shape tucked under a mat of cast-off eelgrass and net, the edge of a crate with the clean lines of a hardware store but the smell of something wrong.

Sharma raised a fist. Stop. She went forward alone, weight on the balls of her feet, and used Mark's multi-tool to tease the net away. The crate lid had been screwed shut and then taped for weather. Stenciled across one side, a black spray-paint code: ORCHID-R / 23-F.

Sophie filmed. She didn't realize she'd been holding her breath again until she saw Paws's flank move in the frame and remembered air.

Voices feathered the reeds. Two men, not careful because they had never had to be. They were close—closer than Mark's sense of self-preservation liked.

Sharma's whisper was almost inaudible. "Back into the grass. Now." She pointed, shoved, shepherded. Paws slid with them, a ghost of gold.

Two figures emerged with the casual confidence of people who believe the world has always bent for them. One carried a toolbox. The other had a canvas duffel slung across his back and the kind of grin that doesn't come from anything wholesome. The duffel clinked. The toolbox made a different sound—densely packed, metallic, organized.

"Pop it and let's split," the toolbox man said. "We're losing water."

"After *that*?" the other said, jerking his chin toward the mouth of the cove where the drone's lights had been visible earlier. "We wait it out. We get under."

"We don't sit on product," toolbox said, and knelt by the crate.

Sharma moved before he could. She stepped out with a strange kind of calm, hand up, voice even. "Stop right there."

Men whose lives had taught them to run tried to run. One went left and hit sucking mud; the other went right and hit Paws.

The dog does not maul or cripple; he impedes. He grabbed the duffel strap and sat down. The man stumbled, swore, flailed for the pack. Paws leaned back, unyielding as a boat cleat. Mark was on the man a heartbeat later, not to harm but to stop. They crashed into grass. Cold black mud took them both up to the shin.

The toolbox man spun back with something that looked like a crowbar. Sophie's mouth opened on a warning that came out as a squeak. Sharma didn't shoot—this was a marsh full of ricochets—but she moved like someone who had done this before. She pushed the crowbar away with one hand and pulled the man toward her with the other, flipped him neatly, and let the marsh take some fight out of him before the zip tie did the rest.

Mark's man tried to elbow him low. Mark grunted, teeth clacking hard enough to ring, and saw stars. Then he saw Paws plant his front paws, set his legs, and become a fulcrum. The duffel strap came free with a wet snap. The man turned to bolt and met a knee from Sharma that changed his mind. He went still long enough for plastic to sing around his wrists.

"Everyone breathing?" Sharma asked, almost cheerful in the adrenaline afterglow.

"Mostly," Mark said. He glanced at the duffel. "That felt like metal."

"It sounds like evidence," Sharma said, and knelt. The zipper turned and stuttered on grit before giving. Inside lay length upon length of ghost net—thin, nearly invisible monofilament designed to fish whether a human was there or not. It kills without anyone to witness. Beneath the net, wrapped in oilcloth, were four gallon jugs of a viscous amber liquid labeled in black marker with a code that matched the crate: ORCHID-R. At the very bottom: a cheap burner phone still on and the flashing light of a message.

Sharma pressed her lips. "We'll bag it," she said. To Sophie: "Get me a timestamp and a shot of the unread message screen."

Sophie leaned in. The preview showed only a fragment: Shift ports to South Inlet; marsh drop confirms. B.E. sign-off secured. —A.

"B.E.," Mark said. "Beacon... something? Or initials."

"Or both," Sharma said. She sealed the bag and then crouched by Paws, bringing the field kit out again to check the earlier cut. The gauze was spotted but no longer seeping. Paws held her gaze and accepted the pat with dignity. "You're getting steak," she told him. "Approved by the State."

They worked fast. Mark tied a flagging tab every twenty yards as they retraced their path. Sophie, trembling finally in the come-down, found her humor. "Next time we go for a walk," she whispered to Paws, "we're taking the sidewalk."

By the time they hiked back to the cove, dawn was lifting the world from charcoal to charcoal-blue. The cutter's lights had moved seaward, towing a small boat that sat sullen and listing, engines useless and pride punctured. On the beach, the canisters waited where they'd been photographed and tagged. The satchel lay in a sealed bag. The lookout sat on his heels with his hands behind him, Ranger Jenkins standing easy at his shoulder and not missing a single breath he took.

A forensic tech team in white Tyvek moved in a choreography that looked like care made visible: swabs, vials, tweezers, click and seal, bag and tag. They were quiet. Science in the wild asks for that.

The Rangers lifted four sea turtles out of the small cabin of the grounded go-fast hours later—two juvenile greens and two loggerheads, their shells dulled by oil sheen but their eyes bright and angry at being caged. They were transferred to padded tubs for triage and transport. The rest of what they found turned the night's arrest into the spine of a case: undersize nets, illegal traps, hooks without escape vents, and inside the bow locker, two more of the stainless canisters.

Ranger Hayes took the satchel in his hands last. He read the note and was still for the length of two heartbeats. Then he placed the envelope where the chain-of-custody form said it had to be and looked up at Mark and Sophie.

"You did exactly what I needed you to do," he said, simple praise without decoration. His eyes softened when he looked at Paws. "He did more."

Sophie laughed once, a short bright sound she hadn't known she had left. "He wants to pretend he didn't," she said, pressing her face into Paws's neck for a second. The dog leaned into her, the universal gesture that says *you are mine and I am yours.*

Hayes's radio barked a final time. "Cutter Argent to Ranger Hayes—suspects transferred, hull secured for tow, evidence logged per boarding report. We'll transmit files within the hour."

"Copy, Argent. Appreciate the dance," Hayes said. He turned back to the cove. "Silas, you still with me?"

"Aye," came the answer, rough as rope. "The skiff boys didn't make their getaway. Saw a flicker of activity up the marsh, then nothing. Guess they got their feet stuck—happens when you don't belong to the mud. You got what you needed?"

Hayes looked at the crate marked ORCHID-R, at the duffel of ghost net, at the vials of dark fluid, at the note trembling under the weight of consequences. He looked at a dog with a line of clean gauze on his shoulder and sand on his whiskers. "I think we did," he said.

By the time the first honest blush of day put color in the clouds, the cove looked almost like itself again. Almost. Boot prints braided with bird tracks.

A few flagged stakes stuck out of the sand where measurements had been taken. The smell of solvent rose even as the wind freshened, as if the things humans do to water want to announce themselves as long as they can.

Neighbors watched from a distance, eyes serious and mouths careful. Teenagers who'd spent the night flashing coded signals in the scrub sat on their heels now, yawning with relief. Mrs. Gable stood with a tray of pastries she must have started in the dark, steam curling up into the soft air. Old Mr. Henderson leaned on his cane and seemed taller than he'd been yesterday.

Officer Sharma handed Sophie a sealed bag with a clean copy of a single photo she'd taken without being asked: the canisters on the sand, the satchel unzipped to show the rolled maps, Paws's nose in the frame because Paws is always in the frame. "For your records," Sharma said. "For your courage."

Sophie's eyes pricked. She tucked the photo inside her jacket like it was a live thing that might fly if she wasn't careful.

Mark took a last look at the laminated card with its printed formulae, the logo, the phone number, and the back with grit ground into it. He didn't burn the whistleblower's note when he wanted to. He would, after copies and protocols, because that was the safer way to honor its instruction. But for a second he let himself imagine the person who had written it—someone with ink on their fingers and the shape of fear sitting behind their sternum. *We are not all dirty.*

He looked at Sophie, who was feeding Paws a contraband corner of croissant offered by Mrs. Gable. He looked at Officer Sharma, mud to the knee and eyes bright. He looked at the marsh, at the thin silver trickles of last tide running out, at the faint path of a skiff cut through grass and already healing.

Heron's Cove exhaled with them.

The arrests would be headlines; the crates would be evidence; the Coast Guard's log would go to a case file; a judge would weigh what had been taken and what might be taken still. But the moments that would keep breathing in the Reynolds house were quieter: a dog's shoulder under a child's hand; the feel of a satchel too heavy with proof; the sight of a turtle's face when it realized a lid had opened and sky still existed.

Hayes let his team finish their work and then stood alone at the water's edge long enough to let the waves take the tip of his boots. He thought of the word *Serpent* and how humans always name hazards after things with teeth when so many hazards arrive on pallets marked with clip art. He thought of the initials on the burner phone and the name in the note. He thought of the phone call he would make later to a contact at the state attorney's office that would begin with *I need a quiet ear.*

Behind him, voices braided with gulls. He turned back to the living.

"Heron's Cove secured," he said into the radio, but also to himself, but also to the place. "Canisters, maps, digital storage, secondary cache in marsh recovered. One lookout and two marsh runners in custody. Primary vessel disabled and boarded. Wildlife triage in progress. We're going to need bigger boxes for the next part."

On the dune, Mark and Sophie watched the sun find the carved lines of water on sand and turned to go when Paws did. The dog's gait had the faint stiffness of a shallow cut and a long night and the kind of pride that made his tail carry a notch higher. Sophie brushed sand from his ears and whispered something only he needed to hear.

They climbed the path together, three sets of footprints and a trail of flagging tape bright against the green, leading back toward other chapters they had not yet written. The air still carried a wrongness under the clean salt—evidence has a smell—but it also carried something else, thin and bright as first light: the sense that even in the places where people have decided to be careless, there are always other people who decide the opposite.

At the top of the dune, Sophie looked back at the cove and then toward the maze of marsh where the skiff had been, where a duffel had come loose and a dog had sat his ground and a ranger had moved like water. "Dad?" she said as Paws nosed her hand. "Do you think they'll come back?"

Mark took a breath that filled his ribs with both answer and question. "Maybe," he said. "Or maybe someone else will instead. Either way, we'll be here."

Paws stretched, sighed, and set his paws toward home. The day opened like a tide in the other direction. The night had given them maps and names and wounds and work. It had given them a note from a stranger who might be a friend. It had given them a story with a beginning and a middle and, if they kept walking, the possibility of reaching an ending that looked like more turtles than traps, more water than waste.

They kept walking.

Chapter 10
HEALING AND REFLECTION

By the time the first pink rinsed along the horizon, Heron's Cove looked like a crime scene diagram brought to life. White-suited techs moved in measured patterns; orange flags stippled the sand where swabs had touched oily sheens; camera shutters stitched a quiet rhythm under the gulls. The cutter's drone still hovered in a lazy grid over the Serpent's Tongue, its hum just audible when the surf inhaled. Someone had planted a collapsible "MEDIA LINE — DO NOT CROSS" sign at the top of the access path, but the local paper's stringer was there anyway, lens hungry from fifty feet back.

Paws wore a tidy square of gauze and vet tape over the nick on his shoulder and a look that suggested he was tolerating the attention only because Sophie's palm stayed hooked in his ruff. He stood as still as he could for Ranger Jenkins's second check, flinched once when the alcohol hit, and then leaned, deliberately, into Sophie's knee.

"Surface cut," Jenkins said, rewrapping. "He'll be sore, not limited. I'll have Dr. Patel look him over at the van."

They watched, together, as four juvenile turtles were lifted from the impounded go-fast's cabin—two greens, two loggerheads—each placed in a padded tub like crown jewels that had been kept somewhere they didn't belong. A tech brushed an oily film off a shell with motions that looked like apology made tactile.

Mark kept his eyes on the work and his hands on practical things: photographs, coordinates, the small notebook recovered from the satchel. Sophie had already shot its pages—lines of numbers, arrows to hand-drawn sandbars, words that read like someone had been talking to themselves: deliveries, clients, South Inlet, drop at dead low. On the inside flap: the waste contractor logo she'd pegged in the dark and a string of initials where a name should be.

Ranger Hayes came over with a printout that had the unmistakable look of something just spit from a thermal printer. "Argent's boarding log, preliminary," he said. "Two in custody at the Tongue. Your lookout and the marsh runners make five. The skiff up-estuary? We found it sunk to the gunwales in eelgrass. No souls aboard when we arrived—just footprints to nowhere and a crate exactly like the one you found, empty."

He let the weight of it settle, then added, "State lab's on call. We'll fast-track residue from the canisters and those vials. If it matches the pollutant we've been seeing on the nests, it ties a bow we've needed for a year."

"And the note?" Sarah asked. She stood with her arms crossed in that way she did when she wanted her hands to be useful and there was nothing appropriate to hold. "The envelope—'ask for Inez'?"

Hayes glanced toward the satchel sealed in evidence plastic. "It's real enough. We'll paper it properly before we put anyone at risk. Until then, that name lives in my pocket and nowhere else." He tapped the folder. "And this text from the burner—'B.E. sign-off secured'? If 'B.E.' is Beacon Reclamation...or a person...we tread carefully. They'll have counsel and friends. We do this clean, or we don't do it at all."

He didn't have to say the rest. Everyone standing there had lived in the world long enough to know what happens when money and waste share a handshake.

By mid-morning, the cove had exhaled most of its urgency. The techs packed their kits like field surgeons; the Coast Guard cut loose the tow; the rangers swapped radios for clipboards. The community edged closer. Mrs. Gable set a tray of still-warm buns on the tailgate of a Parks truck like a flag of truce in a long war. Old Mr. Henderson shook Hayes's hand with both of his and muttered something that sounded like "'Bout time someone snapped the line."

A Parks van ferried the turtles to the rehab center two towns over. The van next to it carried Paws and Sophie to Dr. Patel—just to be sure, Jenkins said, and really so Sophie could replace the adrenaline with doing.

The mobile clinic smelled like disinfectant and canned pumpkin, a standard-issue canine currency. Dr. Patel, unflappable in scrubs patterned with tiny paw prints, knelt to Paws's level and performed the kind of exam that looks like affection doing detective work.

"He's fine," Dr. Patel said, after cleaning and closing the cut more neatly. "No stitches. Keep the bandage dry as possible." She smiled at Sophie in a way that landed. "He protected you. That's a job that pulls on everything—body and brain. Let him sleep as much as he wants today. He'll tell you when he wants more."

Sophie nodded. She'd been iron-spined through the night but now felt marsh-soft around the edges. She pressed her face into Paws's neck for a count of three. He breathed in her hair and made a noise that was almost a hum.

On a side table, a rehab tech worked a Q-tip gently around a rescued gull's beak to remove a line of gluey sheen. In the corner, a poster showed hatchling turtles arrowing toward dawn. Sophie stood before it and memorized the exact angle of their little flippers.

Home was quiet in the way of a house that had held too much sound. They showered until the water ran cool, stuffed salt-stiff clothes in a bag, and ate whatever Mrs. Gable had wrapped in foil. The TV on the counter bled low-volume local news into the kitchen: a stock photo of the beach, a voice-over about a "joint operation," a blurred shot of flashing lights across water. No names. No addresses. Yet.

While Leo napped on the sofa with one hand in Paws's fur—everyone pretending the hand wasn't there in case he woke and remembered it wasn't—Mark and

Sarah sat at the table with Hayes's card and the notebook open between them. The adrenaline valley turned the edges of everything too sharp.

"You're thinking about the maps and the drive," Sarah said.

"I'm thinking about the maps and the drive," Mark said. "And about the burner phone message. South Inlet. B.E. And about how the Tongue has been chewing boats since before I could walk, and they still tried it—that means either panic or arrogance. Or both."

Sarah traced a line of numbers with her nail. "Or confidence that, even if they lost one boat, the rest of the operation keeps moving. That's what scares me. We hit one artery. How many are there?"

He didn't answer, because the landline rang for the first time in a month and there are some superstitions you don't state out loud.

"Reynolds residence," Mark said, because that was who he was when the landline rang.

"Mr. Reynolds, Officer Sharma," came the warm, clipped voice. "Two things. One, preliminary lab swabs from the canisters are a likely match for the pollutant we've been seeing at the nesting sites—early, but strong. It's not just oil; it's cocktail. We'll get the full list, but it's our link. Two"—her tone softened around the edges—"I'm calling about your family. The Parks Foundation and a few other orgs have arranged targeted aid. Anonymous donors. It's intended for families who've borne tangible costs from these crimes. It's not charity with strings. It's insulation: veterinary bills, your lost hours, replacing that busted back door you still haven't fixed. You're on the list. If you're willing."

Sarah had pressed the speaker button at Sharma's name and now let out a sound that managed to be both laugh and breath. "We...we don't even know what to say."

"'Thank you' is customary," Sharma said dryly, and then gentled it further. "Also 'yes.' Paperwork will come through the Foundation. If anyone asks you to sign something weird, call me first. We know how to read 'weird.'"

After they hung up, the kitchen filled with a silence that had weight to it.

"It helps," Mark said, and he meant financially, but also that someone had thought to ask: *What did this cost you?* It helped that there were institutions with names that could be printed on the check besides the ones stamped on crates found in marsh grass. But another thought tugged. "What if 'anonymous' is a way of not being publicly tied to us? What if it's someone who will want something later?"

"Or," Sarah said, practical in the way she became when fear tried to get clever, "it's exactly what Sharma said: a clean way to help without turning us into a press release. We accept it for what it is. We keep our eyes open. We keep receipts."

They let themselves feel how it changed the next hour, at least: Paws's follow-up visits didn't sit like stones; the cracked bathroom window could be replaced; the mental math that had been a constant hum quieted half a notch. It didn't solve everything. It made solving possible.

The first blowback came small. That afternoon, Mark noticed a dark SUV idling at the end of their street longer than made sense if you were choosing a radio station. He memorized the plate because fifteen years of small business had taught him what papers don't print. When he went outside to check the mail he found the box askew, the hinge bent. Inside, between the phone bill and a pizza coupon, lay a single business card with nothing but the letters B.E. stamped in an embossed gray that turned metallic in the sun.

When he told Sarah, she nodded like she had always been waiting for something to announce itself. She photographed the card, slid it into a sandwich bag with a strip of paper and the date, and texted the photo to Hayes with *Found in mailbox. Plate of SUV attached. No interaction.*

Hayes wrote back one word—*Logged*—and then, two minutes later, another: *Careful.*

They told Sophie the truth, adjusted for age and for the fact that she had been brave more than enough in the last twenty-four hours. She listened, then patted Paws's side. "He already knows," she said, with a certainty that made Mark's throat get complicated. Paws thumped his tail once like a judge with a gavel.

Healing said it wanted quiet, but the day didn't always give it. When word of the operation finally rippled from porch-to-porch into a town meeting, the community center filled to its fire code with neighbors carrying folding chairs and opinions.

Hayes opened with a brisk summary that left out everything it had to and included everything it could: a suspect vessel grounded and boarded, contraband recovered, wildlife rescued, a strong scientific link under analysis. He thanked the Coast Guard, the forensics team, and "certain citizen partners whose names I won't say because I like their lives just the way they are."

Applause. Relief. Then the questions.

A contractor who'd never shown up to a conservation meeting in his life stood to ask whether "armed raids" on "small-time fishermen" were really the best use of public funds. A woman whose rental cottage sat near the South Inlet asked if the police tape on "her beach" would be down by Saturday.

And then a man in a crisp blazer and boating shoes—who introduced himself as a "regional liaison for Beacon Reclamation" and smiled the way people smile on television—rose to offer "full cooperation to the authorities," which sounded like a denial wrapped in a handshake. "We take any implication of malfeasance very seriously," he said smoothly. "If any of our equipment or branding has been misused, we will investigate vigorously. We are committed to clean water."

Sarah saw the way the room turned its face toward the word Beacon and saw half a dozen different stories catch in half a dozen throats. She stood, surprised to find the microphone in her hand. "If you're committed to clean water," she said, "then you know what our turtle nests looked like in June. You know about the sheen in the wrack line and the fish we saw floating belly-up in the side channel. If someone misused your branding, you should probably ask yourself why the misusers thought it helped. And if no one misused it, then we expect to see your cooperation turn into something we can feel in our lungs and see in our tide pools."

There was a thread of applause—more than a thread. The Beacon man's smile didn't twitch. "We'll be in touch," he said, which wasn't an answer and told everyone everything.

On the drive home, Mark and Sarah didn't speak until the stop sign at the market.

"You were good," Mark said finally. "Measured."

"I wanted not to be," Sarah admitted. "But if we're part of this, we can't burn what the rangers will need later."

"Also," he said, eyes on the rearview, "we can't make ourselves bigger targets than we already are."

They didn't say out loud *We already are* because Paws's ears were at the same angle they used when the oven timer beeped and the wind changed; it felt cruel to give the house another reason to tense.

That night, the first hard dream came for Sophie. That the ocean had turned to syrup. That she was running in it and could not. That a small turtle, eyes older than the moon, tugged at her shirt and whispered, not this way, little one, back to the stars. She woke in the country between shout and breath and found Paws already on the bed with his chin on her ankle, monitoring. He didn't wag; he matched his breathing to hers until the ocean thinned and the room came back with its old familiar edges. In the murk of the hall, Sarah leaned against the doorjamb and remembered the first time she had watched her daughter sleep as a newborn, the same helpless wonder, the same animal vow.

In the morning, Sophie asked if they could "take Paws to his appointment alone," as if the word *appointment* could be fitted over anything that hurt.

At Dr. Patel's clinic, the hallway smelled like oatmeal biscuits again. A tech showed Sophie how to stroke along a muscle line without pressing the tender part; Paws half-closed his eyes, theatrically grateful. Dr. Patel adjusted the bandage and, in the small space before the next patient, said softly to Sarah, "There's a therapy group for kids who've helped in rescues—some of the kids whose families volunteer at the rehab center. It's not dramatic. It's... sharing the way the brain tries to rehearse danger. It can help with the dreams."

Sophie, pretending to read the poster about microchips, listened without turning around. "Can Paws come?" she asked, attempting nonchalance and absolutely failing in the way that breaks adults open with love.

"He'll be the most popular one there," Dr. Patel said.

By the week's end, the first state lab report landed: a string of long names that together formed the chemical signature of the slick that had killed hatchlings in the early part of the season. Matches to the residue swabbed from the canisters. The email went out to Hayes and to the state attorney and—because she'd been added to the list by a ranger without asking—to Officer Sharma, who promptly forwarded a plain-language version to Sarah with the subject line Just to have the words.

They read it at the kitchen table. Leo colored a picture of a very square turtle at the other end like he was taking notes in crayon. Mark's thumb tapped the wood in a pattern he used when he was doing math in his head. The words sat there heavy and simple: the link was made.

"Now what?" Sophie asked.

"Now," Mark said, "we keep saying what we saw. We don't make it bigger. We don't make it smaller. And when people who are paid to make us tired talk, we take turns answering so none of us forgets how to be a person."

Sophie put her palm on Paws's shoulder where the fur was growing back through the shaved patch. "Okay," she said. "But I might let him answer some of the questions."

"You'd get better quotes," Sarah said, and finally laughed, properly, for the first time since the night at the cove.

It was a good thing they took the small wins where they could, because the next week held its share of sand in the gears.

A reporter in a too-neat shirt knocked at odd hours on three consecutive days. A talk radio host framed the operation as "overreach against hardworking watermen," kickstarting a flood of calls from people who used words like "jackboot." A thick man at the grocery store leaned in too close to Mark in the dairy aisle and said, "You got kids, right?" in a tone that was all question and no question at all. The Beacon liaison's office issued a press statement that managed, in 200 words, to sound concerned, litigious, ignorant, and omniscient.

The anonymous donor fund cleared their bank in two disbursements—one marked Parks Foundation and one Coastal Resilience Fund—which meant the bathroom window could be replaced and Paws's therapy was paid ahead for a month and Mark bought a lock for the side gate he had been meaning to buy since spring. It also meant that when a plain envelope with no return address showed up under the windshield wiper of his truck with a printed note—KEEP YOUR DOG ON A LEASH—his first call could be to Sharma, not the part of his brain that liked parking lots after dark. She arrived ten minutes later, read the note, bagged it with a gloved hand, and stood in the driveway with the kind of patience that makes you feel like you're not being watched even when you are.

"People get stupid when they're scared," she said. "People who profited from this are scared. People who don't want to admit they turned their head are scared. Stupid plus scared equals anonymous notes. It also equals mistakes. They'll make some. We'll collect them."

She didn't say *You're not alone* because the car in the cul-de-sac with two rangers in plain clothes already had.

Meanwhile, the beach kept showing up like it always did, and that was the conflict that felt both biggest and smallest: how to live a day while the structure of your days reknit itself around a thing that shouldn't have happened. The first calm evening they tried to let be only that, Sophie and Paws found something anyway—a slick where the freshwater runoff from the neighborhood met the sand, the surface of the little stream catching the light like it had been greased.

Paws sniffed, sneezed once, sat down, and pawed delicately at the water without touching it. Sophie squatted and watched the rainbow fan and reform. Mark found an empty jar in the beach bag, rinsed it with salt water, and took a sample per Hayes's phone instructions—gloves, jar three-quarters full, lid tight, keep it cool. Sarah texted a photo to Jenkins. A tech collected it within the hour with a portable cooler and a grateful nod.

The next morning, Hayes called. "Good catch. Not the same mix as the canisters—lighter, like wash water, not dumping. Might be coming from an auto shop or a boat yard uphill. We'll walk the outfalls. If it's innocent and fixable, great. If it's not, we'll fix who needs fixing."

And there it was, the other kind of conflict—the ones that weren't criminal empires but frayed ropes of small harms knotted into a net. The family's life bent slightly around a new expectation: vigilance wasn't just for the nights when boats ran dark; it was for the days when hoses ran bright.

Sophie started the kids' therapy group at the rehab center on a Wednesday. Six children sat cross-legged in a circle on a rug patterned with cartoon shells, each with a dog or a stuffed version thereof. Paws lay down with the soft drama of a sun worshiper and fell asleep so completely that his snores punctuated a boy's story about a pelican he'd helped disentangle from fishing line. The counselor—a woman with sand-colored hair and a voice that made panic pull up a chair and behave—talked about "how the brain tries to prepare us by replaying," and about giving it something else to do: "name five things you can see, four you can touch, three you can hear…"

Sophie didn't volunteer to speak at first. Then she did, because she heard a girl across the circle describe a dream about "molasses ocean" and recognized her own nightmare given a different sweet. She said, "I don't like when my chest forgets how to work," and the counselor said, "That's a good description," and Paws shifted so his paws touched both her shoes like a circuit closed.

On the drive home, she watched the reeds of the marsh in the back window and decided that if the ocean came back in her sleep, she would name five things before it could turn syrup. She said them out loud, to practice. "Paws's ear. Mom's ring. The red cooler. The way the gulls swear. Dad's… tapping thing."

In the front seat, Mark's hand paused above the steering wheel, caught out, and then resumed its small mathematics. "I do not have a tapping thing," he said, and Sarah snorted.

There were good letters, too. Leo's class wrote to "the Sea Turtles that Live Near Us," dictating to their teacher in that oddly formal tone of six-year-olds: We hope your shells are clean now. We are sorry about the people who forget to be careful. We like your flippers. We are learning to pick up small plastic. One child drew Paws with a cape that read DOGTOR.

Mrs. Gable's niece ran their story on a regional environmental blog, which brought emails from strangers who had different coastlines and the same ache: We're fighting this on the bayou, My dad shut down a discharge pipe in '98, Is there a list for the hearing? The Sunset Beach Preservation folks—newly minted, still figuring out how to run a meeting without three tangents diverging at once—forwarded information about county hearings on stormwater upgrades and asked if Sarah would speak. She said yes and then lay awake half the night because saying yes felt like stepping onto a different kind of boat.

Hayes kept his own promises. He met the state attorney for coffee in a booth where the fake plants had dust and spoke the names that mattered in the careful way men do when they're asking someone to risk their reputation. He called a quiet number and asked for a woman named Inez, and when the person who answered said there was no one by that name, he asked what days they served empanadas even though it was a waste contractor's front desk. Two hours later, a plain envelope slid under his office door with a typed list of invoice numbers and one line written in that same narrow hand: You didn't hear this from me. —I. He made three copies on three machines and then burned the original with a chuckle that had no humor in it.

The Beacon liaison requested a meeting with "concerned citizens to clear the air." Hayes declined politely in writing and impolitely in private. The liaison went on the news with his neat hair and said, "We are cooperating fully." Hayes said nothing and filed for two more warrants.

Two weeks after the night at the cove, they went back down at sunset because not going back is another kind of letting someone take something from you. The sand remembered their feet and gave them back that feeling of being temporary in a place that is permanent enough to foster humility. Paws trotted ahead, sound again, cathedral-quiet where it counted.

"Do you hear it?" Sarah asked, hand around Mark's arm.

"The ocean?" he said.

"The relief," she said. "Like it's leaning off us slowly. Not all the way. But enough that I can hear the gulls without thinking they're telling me something is wrong."

"Maybe they're just swearing at each other," Mark said. "It's a full-time job for gulls."

Sophie found a patch of tide-made lace and traced it with her toe. Leo ran back and forth in swash, counting foamy bubbles as if they were sheep. The lighthouse sent its measured blink along the seam where orange turned to indigo.

"Do you think they'll come back?" Sophie asked, because sometimes you have to say aloud what fear sits on like a hen on an egg.

"Someone will," Mark said, honest because he'd promised to be. "Maybe them. Maybe a different them. But so will we. And the we keeps getting bigger."

Paws stopped, lifted his head, and faced down-coast where the wilder stretch lay, the place he had led them before. His ears made that forward angle they made when the world offered him a smell worth filing. He didn't growl. He didn't pull. He stood, a golden outline against a sky that had finally decided not to be dramatic, and then looked back over his shoulder at Sophie.

"Not tonight," she told him. "Tonight we walk our beach."

He seemed to consider that and then fell into step. Sometimes vigilance looks like following a lead into reeds. Sometimes it looks like walking in a straight line with your family under a sky that is doing its job.

Back at the house, they stowed the trowels and the plant protectors out of habit because habits build worlds. Mark picked up the crowbar he'd never gotten around to putting away—and paused, because for a split second he was back in the marsh with the man's arm and the zip tie and his own breath loud in his head. Paws bumped his leg, back to present. Mark leaned the bar in the corner and, for reasons he would not be able to explain later, placed a hand on the doorframe like you pat the neck of a horse.

On the steps, Sarah looked toward the dunes and then to the little sliver of lane where the SUV had idled days before. "I don't want to become a person who only notices danger," she said.

"You won't," Mark said. "You're fundamentally built for noticing everything."

She laughed, and in the laugh was an ease that hadn't been there even the morning after. "So are you. Even your tapping thing."

"I do not have a—" he started, and stopped, because Sophie had come around the corner with Paws adorned in a towel like a cape and Leo had a bucket not of shells but of assorted microtrash, and the dog had that expression particular to dogs in towels: dignity intact in spite of evidence.

"We're keeping some of the pretty glass," Sophie announced. "The rest goes to the big bin. Paws helped."

"Of course he did," Sarah said, and stroked his towel-hooded head.

They sat there until night had a proper hold of the beach and decided, quietly, to keep doing the small things without letting the big things get all the good words. Healing, it turned out, wasn't one arc but a tide chart: predictable in shape, surprising in detail, subject to wind.

Much later, when the house had set its nighttime creaks and the ocean was a long whisper through the screens, Mark woke to the feeling that the world had tilted somewhere under his ribcage. He lay there and listened. Paws's paws made a soft scritch on the hallway runner; the dog paused at their doorway and exhaled, loud enough to be heard, a sound that said *still here*. Across the hall, Sophie rolled and settled; Leo muttered a word that sounded suspiciously like Dogtor.

Mark reached for Sarah's hand across the sheet and found it reaching for his. Outside, the lighthouse blinked on schedule. In a county office, a file with Beacon's name on it got thicker by one sheet. In the marsh, somewhere near where the crate had been, a heron stood on one leg and regarded the night with that same patient expectation that had brought them—finally—through this one.

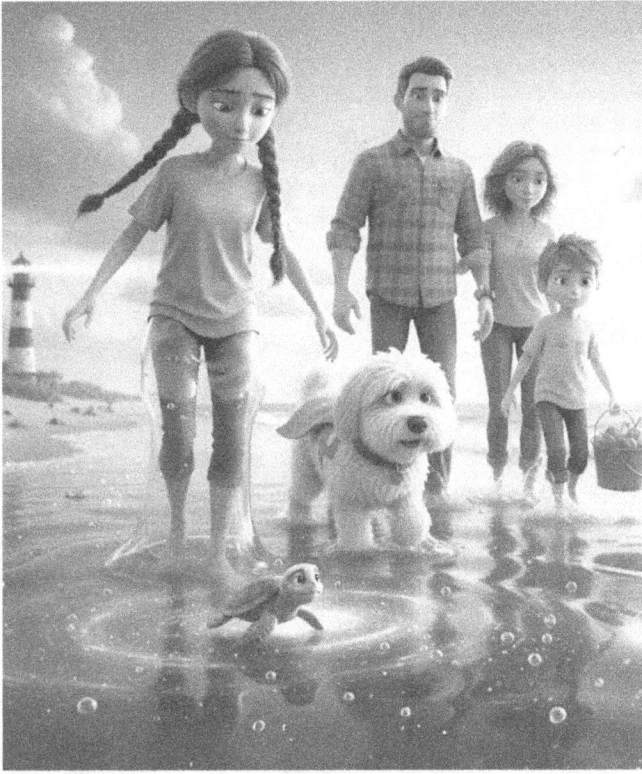

They were not naïve. They were not unafraid. But they had work and a dog and a community that had decided, more days than not, to be brave. The waves brought the day in and took it out again, in the old way. The echoes of the worst of it started to sound like what they had always been: warnings sharpened into promises, heavy things that had already begun to turn into fuel.

Chapter 11
GUARDIANS OF SUNSET BEACH

The first Saturday after the raid, the beach woke to purpose.

They met at the access stairs in mismatched hats and sun-faded shirts, a line of neighbors armed with five-gallon buckets, grabbers, and coffee. Someone had taped a handwritten sign to the rail: COMMUNITY CLEAN—SIGN IN, GLOVE UP, WATCH YOUR TIDE. Paws wove through shins and laces like a small, golden current, pausing for the serious business of having his ears scratched by anyone who looked like they needed it.

Mark handed out zones the way he used to hand out job tickets: south of the jetty to the drift line, wrack to dune toe, the rocky points for people with boots and balance. Sarah ran the table—waivers, a roll of bright flagging tape, a laminated card that listed what *not* to touch. Sophie and Leo had a kid-sized wagon full of empty buckets and a cardboard sign she'd lettered herself: MICROTRASH CREW.

They started slow, the way good habits do. Bottle caps, candy wrappers, a spiderweb of monofilament snagged on sea lavender. The beach looked clean until you let your eyes adjust to the wrong-colored confetti in the sand.

"Check the high line," Sarah called, pointing to the rough ridge of dried weeds and drift. "That's where the small stuff hides."

Paws ranged ahead and toed at a flattened tangle with a delicacy that didn't match his build. He sat, looked back, and pawed once—his "here, please" without the bark. Beneath the wrack: a narrow loop of clear line rigged with a crude slip knot and a short tether to a stake driven just under the surface. It would take a gull or a shorebird by the leg if luck broke mean.

"Snare," Mark said, crouching. He steadied the stake, cut the loop free with the shears from his belt, and lifted the whole thing using the flagging tape to create a bright leash between danger and disposal. "Bag for forensics first," he added, glancing up toward where Ranger Sharma had parked by the stairs.

Sharma was already picking her way down. "Good catch," she said, mood all business, eyes quietly pleased. "We'll run it with the rest. Small harm, big pattern."

"Do you think it's related?" Sarah asked.

"Same coastline, same week, same thinking," Sharma said. "That's enough for me to take it seriously."

Not everything was law and evidence. Some of it was friction you could feel long before it sparked. Two men in ball caps and salt-stained waders came down the sand with rods angled over their shoulders like question marks.

"You folks gonna pick up the fish, too, when you scare 'em off?" one of them asked. The tone wasn't aggressive; it was tired and edged.

Mark kept his voice level. "We're staying below the high line and out of the wash. You keep to the wet sand with hooks down, nobody's in anybody's way."

"County's harassed enough watermen this month," the taller one grumbled. He wasn't looking at Mark. He was looking at the bright evidence bags Sharma carried.

"Different fight," Sharma said. "And we're in it with you when it's about outsiders dumping where you work."

The second man cut his eyes to Paws, who had sat politely and was looking very much like a dog who wanted to be told he was a good dog. The man's posture eased a fraction. "That your dog that found that snare?" he asked Sophie.

"It's a team effort," she said solemnly, and Paws thumped his tail twice, sealing the contract.

They fanned out again. The morning found a rhythm: spot, bag, log; wave at a neighbor; wade into the small hush of a tidepool and place one bottle shard in a bucket like it mattered because it did.

The cleanup was the visible part. The more permanent thing happened that evening over folding chairs and a projector in the community center. Someone brought lemonade. Someone else brought a whiteboard that had last been used for softball signups. The words ENVIRONMENTAL WATCH went up in block letters.

The first meeting was messy. Good messy. People wanted to help. People wanted to argue about what helping looked like. Mark drew a rectangle and labeled it COORDINATION, then smaller rectangles inside—Shoreline Patrol, Data & Reporting, Education, Outreach, Funding, Gear Recovery—because he'd learned long ago that a problem that feels too big can be shrunk by putting it in boxes.

"Shared online hub," Sarah said, writing it on the board. "Photos. Sightings. Schedule. No grandstanding, no shaming—just facts and coordination."

Mrs. Gable, retired teacher and reigning queen of laminated materials, volunteered to moderate the hub. "We'll keep it useful and kind," she said. "Two posts in a row with more heat than light, you sit a week out."

Mr. Henderson raised a hand that had spent seventy years holding a net. "There's gear on the rocks that'll drown a bird or a kid," he said. "Not jobs for bare hands. We'll do a 'recovery day.' Two boats, four old fools who know those ledges, and anyone else who can tie a bowline without YouTube."

"'Gear Recovery' gets its box," Mark said, adding a checkmark.

By the time the chairs scraped back, they had a rotation for sunrise walks, a text tree for hot tips, and a small argument about whether the group should be called Guardians or Stewards. They punted on the name and voted without dissent to meet weekly until the tide of urgency slackened.

At home, Mark built the digital hub after dinner—a simple, private site with a map, a calendar, and a hatchery of color-coded pins. He added a form with three fields: *What did you see? Where? When?* That was it. The rest of the internet could debate. They needed people to look, note, and act.

Their first campaign launched a week later: LEAVE NO TRACE: TAKE ONLY PHOTOS, LEAVE ONLY FOOTPRINTS. The signs were simple and kind, sketched by Sarah and lettered by a teenage artist from the next block. They went in at the access points and at the dune paths. The boards carried a short list in plain language—pack it in/pack it out; stay off the dune grass; keep dogs leashed near nests; cigarette butts are plastic; thank you. At the bottom, a small line: A project of your neighbors at Sunset Beach.

The signs lasted three days.

On the fourth, two were tagged with sloppy marker and one was pulled and left face-down in the scrub.

Sophie found the toppled board on the way back from the inlet with Paws. "Why do people do that?" she demanded, frustration shading her cheeks.

"Sometimes 'Don't' sounds like a dare," Mark said, setting the post upright. "Sometimes people don't like being told anything by a sign. Sometimes they're bored."

They added small trail cameras—low-profile, solar-charged, pointed not at people's faces but at the posts themselves to see who was angry at wood and screws. The footage showed a group of high schoolers, all elbows and energy, using the sign as a bench, then a springboard, then a target for a kick that looked more like indecision than malice.

Sarah could have sent the clip to the school. Instead she showed it to Sophie. "You and Maya know some of them," she said. "You want to handle it?"

Sophie and her friend found the kids at the basketball court and did something adults forget how to do: they asked, without the weight adults put on a question. Why. A redhead with chipped nail polish shrugged. "It's lame," she said. "Like, we already know not to litter."

Sophie didn't argue. "Want to design a better one?" she asked instead. "We'll put your names on it. You can tell us what you actually read, and we'll take off anything you eye-roll at."

Two weeks later, the new signs went up. They were bolder, with fewer words and a simple drawing Paws would not sit still beside long enough to emulate—dog on leash, hand dropping trash in a bag, feet staying off a dune. At the bottom: MADE BY SUNSET BEACH KIDS.

Nobody kicked those.

The pushback that came with letterhead felt different. Two days after the signs went up, an email landed in the hub's inbox from a man whose subject line was Concerns re: Community Overreach. The body was longer and smoother: he supported "personal responsibility," he wrote, but he questioned whether "unauthorized signage" could "confuse visitors" and create "liability." His signature block bore the logo of Beacon Reclamation and the title *Regional Liaison*.

"Here we go," Mark said, dry.

Sarah typed a reply that sounded like a smile with teeth. Thanks for the concern. The signs were installed with Parks' blessing and are purely educational. If your company would like to sponsor additional ash cans and monofilament bins, we'll gladly put your name on those. She cc'd Hayes, Sharma, and the Parks superintendent.

No response, which was its own answer.

When Beacon requested a "listening session," the watch group split. Some wanted the gesture of dialogue; others smelled co-option in the letterhead. They compromised: a public meeting at the community hall, recorded, with questions submitted in writing and read by a neutral moderator.

The liaison arrived with a floral shirt and spotless deck shoes, accompanied by a lawyer who wore a face like a mask. He spoke at length about partnerships, community engagement, and their newly launched Clean Waves Initiative, complete with a glossy trifold showing a smiling family picking up trash at a beach that was definitely not theirs.

"Are you offering money?" someone asked bluntly from the back.

"We're offering alignment," the liaison said smoothly. "Resources can follow."

A murmur went through the room like wind through reeds. Sarah raised her hand and, when the moderator nodded, spoke into the microphone. "We're not a brand," she said. "We're your neighbors with buckets. If you want alignment, we could use a grant for a filter at the outfall by Harbor Lane and five more monofilament bins. We'll put your logo on the back of a recycling container. We won't put it next to the word *guardian*."

The liaison smiled another TV smile. "We'll be in touch."

They were. They offered to sponsor Golden Paws Day, a "family-friendly festival celebrating stewardship," with a stage and a banner big enough to be seen from the highway. The watch group politely declined. They held Dune Day instead, no stage, just a tent with water jugs, a table of native seedlings, a shade tarp for kids, and a line of neighbors marking plantings with popsicle sticks that bore initials and hopes. Paws lay in the shade like a lion with his pride, approving every child who stopped to pat his head.

The watch group's second month felt less like sprinting and more like building something that could last.

Mr. Henderson's "recovery day" pulled a record tangle of orphaned gear from the rocks. Two old-timers clambered goat-sure along a ledge with a throw hook while a younger pair in waders managed the lines. They hauled a heavy clump of net that had been catching everything unlucky enough to swim near it and coiled it into a sad, heavy wreath on the sand. A little boy stared. "We're making the ocean breathe better," Henderson told him, and the boy nodded as if that was science, which it was.

Mark found himself thinking in inches and gallons: how far the water climbed into the dune toe on a strong south blow, how many cigarette butts could be caught by one more ash can by the stairs, how much clean sand a single damaged outfall could turn to glue. He took a day off to meet a county engineer at the Harbor Lane outfall and walked through a plan for a swirl concentrator—a simple, durable filter that would settle grit and catch floaters before they hit the sand. "You show me volunteers to help pour the pad and I'll find you the budget match," the engineer said. "My supervisor's kid came home raving about a dog named Paws. You've got goodwill. Spend it on concrete."

Sarah's sketchbook thickened with studies of the plants they were placing: sea oats, panic grass, seaside goldenrod. She drew the way the stems held sand in the wind, the shallow web of roots that made a net tough as anything built in a shop. She said yes to a talk at the elementary school and built a show-and-tell from shells, seed heads, and stories. She stood under a dim projector and spoke in a voice that made kids sit forward on their carpet squares. "Everything you do out there," she said, pointing toward the windows that showed a rectangle of sky and, beyond that, the invisible sea, "tells the beach what you think of it. It tells the gulls, and the turtles, and the tiny crabs you can't see. What do you want it to hear?"

Sophie's Beach Buddy Brigade met twice a week after homework. Kids in bright shirts with a swirled paw print logo fanned out with grabbers and buckets, building an economy of small victories. They weighed the haul each session and kept a chart on the hub: Ten pounds. Eight pounds. Twelve. Their favorite find was a lost flip-flop that fit nobody and everybody; they turned it into a bird-feeder for the school garden and declared it "art." One afternoon, Paws nosed a wad of seaweed and sat the way he'd learned to sit when something didn't belong. Sophie pulled back the algae and found a limp shape: a small shorebird snagged in a loop of fishing line. She remembered the training from rehab: slow hands, cut the line close, keep the feathers dry. Paws lay very still, head on paws, as if he knew his stillness mattered more than any help his feet could give. The bird shook itself, blinked, and ran—an ungainly miracle.

"Log it," Sophie said, voice shaking a little, and Maya took a photo of nothing but a patch of wet sand where something had been in trouble and wasn't anymore.

Not every day ended in a tidy bow.

Two beach-front owners complained to the county about "unauthorized volunteers" and "traffic." One left a passive-aggressive note on the hub about "self-appointed eco-police." A tourist influencer posted a video titled Locals Harassed Us for Having Fun at Sunset Beach that showed five seconds of a polite sign and two minutes of someone doing cartwheels on a dune. The comment section did what comment sections do. Mark and Sarah learned to let their phones sit in drawers and to answer questions only where answers mattered—in person, at meetings.

One evening, Paws alerted at the Harbor Lane stream again. Oil rainbow, faint but there. The auto shop uphill had been warned; they claimed they'd changed their practices; the data said otherwise. Mark walked the storm drains with a county inspector who wore boots and an expression like a man done having his time wasted. They found a cross-connection—someone had tied a wash bay into a drain marked with a fish symbol without thinking about what a fish means.

Fixing it took a week, three calls, two threats of a fine, and finally, a posted notice. The shop owner came to the next watch meeting red-faced and defensive and left with an offer to pay for the Harbor Lane filter. He signed the check in a hand that looked like a storm blown over and shook Mark's hand hard.

"Sometimes people need a lever," Sarah said softly as they rolled the filter into place. "We got one. Let's use it for good."

They did. The hub lit with small wins: a nest fenced and left in peace; a monofilament tube full to overflowing; a photo of a pod of dolphins in crisp morning light that made the work feel like a hymn.

King tides crested in late month, glassy and implacable. The ocean climbed the slope and stroked the new dune toe like a big hand. The planted sea oats bowed and held. When the water fell back, it left a clean line, the sand cut but not gutted. Mark walked the length with a tape, measuring the scarp where the old, weak grass had given way and the slow, proud places where the new plantings had held like stitched seams.

"It's working," he said, a statement and a promise.

"It's beginning," Sarah corrected, smiling. "Working is a word for next year."

They knew beginning meant repetition. So they planned. The hub's calendar filled: Gear Day II; Monofilament Monday; Leave No Trace sign refresh; School field trip; Hearing—Stormwater Improvements—County Hall. The last one made Mark's stomach do a small acrobatic flip like a fish clearing the surface. He wrote his three minutes in neat block print and read them to the kitchen. Sarah red-penned the part where he called a consultant's report "uninspired" and suggested "insufficient" instead. He sighed and admitted she was right.

At night they were as tired as deckhands and slept like people who had done something undeniably useful with their hands. When the old fear crept up the stairs, it found the rooms occupied: Leo snoring into Paws's flank; Sophie penning Beach Buddy Bulletin for the hub; Sarah washing sand out of her hair at the kitchen sink; Mark sketching a cross-section of an outfall that made his engineer's brain purr.

They argued sometimes. About how much time they were spending at meetings. About whether to accept a donation from a business owned by the cousin of a man they didn't care to owe. About how many nights a week were allowed to be french-toast-for-dinner nights before someone had to cook a vegetable. They said sorry. They redistributed chores like adults. They learned the sound of each other's fatigue and cut conversations short before words were said that would take too much sand to bury.

Paws wove through it like a string, holding them all on the same line. He woke Mark early and made him walk before email could take his morning hostage. He blinked slow at Sarah until she sat at the edge of the deck and watched a pelican land with more grace than physics should allow. He stood in front of Sophie on mornings when her cheer pulled too tight and pressed his head into her knees until she laughed and the tightness let go. He gave Leo permission to be messy and loud and small and to learn that caring for a place doesn't mean you can't build an elaborate stick fort and knock it down at high tide just to watch the water carry it away.

He was not a symbol in those moments. He was a dog, damp and sandy and ridiculous and perfect. The symbol came later, when the town printed DOG WASTE = WATER WASTE cards with his picture on them, and when kids started pointing and whispering, "That's the beach dog," with the same reverence they used to reserve for firefighters and ice cream trucks.

By the third month, the watch group's meetings had changed shape. They started on time, ended on time, and included a five-minute report from each sub-group. Data & Reporting had built a simple dashboard that showed pounds collected, incidents logged, and a running "oats count" for new plantings. Outreach had a rotation for schools and a schedule for market days with a cheerful table and a bucket full of bottle caps that kids could plunge their hands into while someone explained how many little round plastic things make a big problem.

Funding had become a real committee. They opened a small community account with triple signers, posted quarterly reports on the hub, and set rules that would have satisfied the pickiest auditor. They ran a bake sale that produced too many brownies and exactly the right number of dollars. They sold simple shirts with SUNSET BEACH GUARDIANS around a little wave and a paw print, and when someone pointed out that *Guardians* had won the naming vote by two, the Stewards faction conceded with good humor and the suggestion that Stewards made a better name for the next grant.

Gear Recovery found a rhythm and a following. Pictures of the big hauls became their own genre:

nets rolled tight and zip-tied like sleeping whales; lead weights neatly sorted by size; the strangest object of the week (a lawn chair, a traffic cone, a purple tricycle). They kept a tally of hooks pulled from the rocks in a jar on the community hall's front desk. Kids shook it and listened to the rattle like a dangerous maraca.

Education was where Sarah lived. She and Mrs. Gable designed a set of laminated cards you could take on a walk: WHAT'S THIS PLANT? WHOSE TRACKS? IS THIS TRASH? with a last panel that said IF IN DOUBT, PACK IT OUT with a little drawing of Paws carrying a bottle in his mouth. They wrote a small grant application for a pilot weekend program that would bring a handful of kids to the tide pools with clipboards and curiosity. They called it Low Tide Labs. It was science without lab coats, and it felt like a church they could bring anyone to.

Shoreline Patrol stayed the heart of it. At sunrise and before dusk, pairs with buckets and grabbers made the slow, quiet walk, eyes tuned to the wrong color, the wrong shape, the wrong smell. They picked up more than trash. They picked up rumors, too—the ones you can only hear when you're moving at a human pace and not staring at your phone. They heard about a boat that sat too low in the water after midnight, about a man no one knew who parked at the far end of Harbor Lane every Tuesday, about an ATV trail scarring the back of the dunes where kids had been daring each other to race.

Sometimes a patrol was just a walk in the most beautiful place they knew. Sometimes it was a call to Sharma and a license plate texted in a pre-set format. Either way, it was a declaration: we're looking.

The county hearing on stormwater upgrades was the kind of civic moment that usually happens in fluorescent light and dies there. This one felt different.

They filled two rows, not in matching shirts, not chanting, just present. Mark stepped to the microphone when his name was called and said his name for the record in a voice that didn't shake.

"I build things that live near water," he said. "I know what a budget looks like. I also know what a filter costs compared to what a dead cove costs. You've got a willing public. We'll meet you with sweat equity and dollars. We're asking you to meet us with a plan that replaces outfalls older than me and a schedule that doesn't end when the news cycle does. I brought a drawing. It's simple. We're not reinventing anything. We're just deciding to care in a way that shows up in the water."

He held up the drawing—clear, clean, understandable. He used the word insufficient once, carefully. He used possible three times, deliberately. A commissioner who had previously worn the expression of a man sitting through a long dental procedure leaned forward for the first time and asked the engineer for the match funds number out loud.

Sarah followed with the kind of three minutes that set the tone of a room. She talked about sea oats and kids and the way the tide line looks after a south wind. She told the story of a small, patient dog who sat next to a small, patient girl while she cut a fishing line to save a bird. She didn't point to the Beacon liaison in the back row. She pointed to an easel where she'd taped a photo—a rust-streaked outfall, rainbow on its surface—jarring not because it was dramatic but because it was ordinary. "This is what you can fix," she said. "This is the part you own. We'll meet you there."

They didn't get everything they asked for. That's not how fluorescent rooms work. They got a pilot on Harbor Lane and two others earmarked for later in the year. They got a public promise to work with the citizen group. They got the contact info of a staffer with actual power and the kind of eyes that said *I grew up near water, too.*

On the way out, the Beacon liaison found them in the hall. "Impressive," he said, smooth as ever. "If you're ready to scale, we can help."

"Help like filters?" Sarah asked.

"Help like resources and messaging," he said. "Partners."

"We have partners," she said, and let the door close between them and the sunset.

That night, Mark and Sarah ate standing up in the kitchen, the way they used to when the kids were tiny and the heat of the day lived in the house's bones. Paws lay with his head on Sarah's foot, warm and grounding. Sophie sprawled at the table, drafting a handout for Low Tide Labs with careful lettering and a small drawing of a crab that looked smug and accurate. Leo built a city of shells on a baking sheet and named the streets after fish.

"Did we do okay?" Mark asked, not because he didn't know but because sometimes it felt good to say the question into the air and hear it bounce off someone you trust.

"You were perfect," Sarah said. "You didn't call anyone's report 'lazy.' You said 'insufficient' like it was a favor."

"I'm teachable," he said, which made her smile in a way that felt like summer.

In the living room, the hub chimed with new pins—photos from patrol, a note that the outfall install date had been set, a reminder about Gear Day II. A private message blinked from the county engineer: Pad pour Saturday? I'll bring the float. Heard good things about your dog.

Paws stretched and sighed, contentment knocking a faint echo out of the floorboards.

"Tomorrow," Sarah said, "we do the Harbor Lane pad and finish the new signs and—"

"And you take an hour with your sketchbook," Mark cut in gently. "And I take Leo to the inlet with the net. And Sophie gets an afternoon that does not include a single meeting."

Sophie looked up, feigning outrage. "What if I *want* a meeting?"

"You can have a meeting with a tidepool," Sarah said. "Agenda: crabs."

They laughed, and then they didn't talk for a while because the house made that evening sound it made when the ocean was close and the wind had decided to be their friend.

Out on the porch, the dune grass whispered a report: still here, still holding. Farther off, the low roll of the surf spelled out the old word in a language that never needed signs: come back tomorrow.

They would. They were Guardians now—not by proclamation, not because anyone had given them a title or a trifold, but because they had taken up a task and stuck with it. The work wasn't glamorous. It was a list on a whiteboard with a coffee ring at the corner and sand stuck in the tape. It was a bucket with a cracked handle and a dog who knew when to sit and when to go.

It was enough. And it was only the beginning.

Chapter 12
ECHOES OF THE WAVES

By now the evening ritual felt like muscle memory—bare feet in cooling sand, the sky bruising to indigo, Paws stretched long as a log at Sophie's shins. But habit didn't make them blind. The night after the county hearing, Mark's head turned at once: two stark lines of ATV treads cut straight up the dune face like slashes, ending in a churned patch the size of

Paws lifted his head, nose working. He rose without hurry but with attention, that coiled, quiet readiness he had when something wasn't right.

"Stay," Mark told Sophie, then started up the slope, planting his feet in the old footprints to spare the grass. At the crest he crouched, fingers brushing the sand. The tracks overlapped small three-toed prints peppered like confetti—plover. Crushed in places. A shallow scrape, kicked-in, where a nest should have been.

Sarah caught up, breath thin. "Do you see—?"

"No shells," Mark said. "Maybe a scrape without eggs yet. Maybe."

Paws nosed the disturbed sand, then sat down abruptly and looked back at them: his alert when he wanted humans, not heroics.

"Call Sharma," Sarah said, voice clipped and professional in a way that meant the soft part of her had gone somewhere safe for a minute.

Ranger Sharma arrived with an LED lamp and the kind of patience that reads as steel. She photographed everything: the tracks, the crushed grass, the rake pattern of the tires where the rider had spun to look back down his damage and floor it again. "We'll shift patrol times," she said, scribbling. "Weeknights after eleven. Word travels. They like to race when nobody's watching."

"We're watching," Mark said.

"Good," Sharma replied. "Then don't chase. Call. We'll chase."

The watch group's hub pinged steady for three days—sightings of night riders, a plate number, a blurry frame from a trail cam that caught a helmet's reflective stripe like a guilty comet. The deputies ran down one teenager, then another, both with parents suddenly surprised to learn that "boys being boys" could carry misdemeanor fines and community service picking up trash under the eyes of the people they'd aggravated.

You'd think that would cool tempers. Instead, tempers found new heat.

A trio of would-be "adventure vloggers" rolled into town with a drone and a thirst for content. They posted a video of themselves "testing erosion" by sprinting up a dune and sliding down on boards. In the comments, they called locals "fun police" and tagged the beach with a hashtag they made up on the spot: #DuneJumpsNotDoom.

Sophie saw the clip because every seventh grader did. At lunch she found the ringleader hunched over his phone outside the deli, a half-formed apology already in his posture when he clocked her expression.

"You got your views," she said, calm but not kind. "Now come fix it."

"Relax," he said. "We were raising awareness."

"Of what?" she asked. "Gravity?"

Paws stood at her knee, tail stiff, eyes never leaving the boy's face. There was nothing threatening in him except the certainty that he belonged here and that she did, too.

In the end, the boys came. They stood in a line and dug new fence posts and listened while Mrs. Gable explained why sea oats aren't there to be pretty. A hundred thousand views bought a Saturday morning with blisters. Sophie took a photo only of their hands on the shovel, tagged nothing, and posted it to the hub with one sentence: Do better, then be quiet.

Beacon Reclamation, graceful as ever, picked a different lane. Two weeks after the hearing, Sarah received a thin, expensive letter from a firm whose name sounded like granite and glass.

Dear Ms. Reynolds— it began, then used a lot of words to say stop saying our client pollutes or we will consider all remedies.

"SLAPP," Mark said, handing it back to her with two fingers like it stung. "Strategic Lawsuit Against Public Participation. They're trying to scare us into shutting up."

Sarah read it again, more slowly. She felt a heat rise that wasn't fear. "I said the outfall was leaking oil," she said. "We tested it. It was."

"Yes," Mark said. "And yes."

They called an environmental lawyer whose card lived stuck to the fridge with a magnet shaped like a sardine. She listened, asked for the letter, then asked for the test results, the photos, the dates, the email from the county engineer who had thanked them for their persistence.

"It's a bluff," she said finally. "But bluffs work if you don't call them. I'll send a note. You also need anti-SLAPP protection at the state level. That takes years. Until then, you have truth and process. Keep both."

The watch group voted to post the letter, minus names, with a basic explainer: If you're threatened for advocating in good faith, tell someone. Then keep advocating. It didn't go viral. It didn't need to.

People who needed to see it saw it, and their backs straightened.

Beacon didn't write again. They started a glossy ad campaign about their "Clean Waves" program instead. Paws appeared on none of the posters.

Hatchlings misorient at lights you can't even see as light until somebody teaches you to look. Two weeks later, somebody's rental wedding lit the beach like noon. The venue had a legitimate permit for music until ten, for a tent on the boardwalk—legitimate for everything but biology. The DJ's uplights threw a candy-colored haze that turned the sand to a runway.

Sophie saw it first, standing on the porch with Paws while Mark loaded the truck for Low Tide Labs in the morning. A smear of movement at the edge of the dark: a scatter of bright coins that weren't coins. Hatchlings—dozens, then more—heading away from the water, toward the pastel glow.

"Mom!" she shouted.

They'd practiced this. Red filters over headlamps. Hands low. No loud voices. The last instruction—*breathe*—was the hardest.

Sarah sprinted to the rental coordinator. "Kill the lights," she said, polite as a blade.

"We have a permit," the coordinator said, a practiced smile pinned to her face.

"You don't have a permit to scramble protected hatchlings," Sarah said. Behind her, Paws let out one sharp bark that made heads turn under the tent. He wasn't menacing; he was punctuation.

The coordinator wavered. The DJ's lights flickered, then went down to a syrupy purple that was better than nothing and still not nearly enough.

"Turn them off," Mark said, arriving with red lens caps, his voice carrying the weight of a man way past asking nicely. "Or Ranger Sharma turns them off."

That name held. The lights died. The music softened to a dull, human murmur.

In the dim, the world snapped into its right geometry. Waves brighter than land. A path the size of a back yard that meant life or not. They worked in a slow line—Mark on one flank, Sarah on the other, Sophie in the middle with Paws glued to her knee, solid and silent. He stayed leashed and out of the sand where the nests lay. He did not herd; he did not touch. He simply pressed against Sophie like an anchor while she crouched and blocked misoriented hatchlings with her hands, turning them gently, letting the ocean draw them the way it had drawn everything here from the beginning.

"Drain, drain," Mark called softly.

At the storm grate a dozen more hatchlings had dropped into the grid of metal and were pinwheeling against the bars, frantic, unfamiliar with the concept of down. Mark lay flat, shoulders wedged, and hooked his fingers behind their tiny, frantic flippers, passing them one by one to Sarah. She cupped each in her palm like a secret and set it on the sand facing home. Paws stared, not blinking, statue-still, as if he understood that even the exhale mattered.

By the time Sharma arrived, there were only two hatchlings left to point, one for Sophie, one for Leo—woken in a swirl of sleepy urgency and now wide-eyed with a kid's particular brand of reverence. The last visible back dipped into the black. Sophie's shoulders finally dropped.

Sharma cited the venue on the spot and radioed for a wildlife team to monitor the site until midnight. "You did it right," she said to Sophie. "All of it."

The coordinator approached, small now. "I'm... sorry," she said.

"Be louder before the problem," Sarah said, not unkind.

The next morning, the hub posted a new resource: Lights Out During Hatch Season. The venue reached out two days later with a photo of new red bulbs and a promise to send a Save the Hatchlings donation with every booking. Sophie accepted the apology with a nod and relief and made Paws a red bandana for hatch nights.

Not every hazard was dramatic. A week after Dune Day II, Paws came in from patrol and held his front paw oddly, like he was thinking about where to put it. Sophie saw the hitch and saw her heart fall through the floor at the same time.

"Let me see," she whispered, kneeling. Paws offered the paw without fuss. A barbed treble hook sat like a nasty thought in the pad, one barb set, two kissing skin.

Mark and Sarah moved like a unit that had practiced for this and had hoped never to use it. They muzzled gently—not because Paws would bite but because pain makes saints swear. Mark slid the hook with a hemostat, backing barbs free with the slow, stupid patience that injuries demand. Sarah flushed the puncture with saline, pressed sterile gauze, and tried very hard not to narrate in a soothing tone that was more for herself than the dog.

Paws didn't yelp. He breathed, slow and focused. He licked Sophie's wrist twice after the bandage was wrapped, a ritual that belonged to just them.

The vet gave him a tetanus update, antibiotics, and a comically small bootie he tolerated the way he tolerated bath time and thunder: with dignity and a grudge that evaporated fast.

Sophie wore the hook on a length of red cord around her neck for the rest of the week—a sharp reminder and a promise. She added more monofilament tubes to the access points and recruited three more kids to check them daily. The jar of recovered hooks at the community hall grew heavy and ugly and satisfying.

The secluded cove kept its secrets long enough to feel like a lullaby, then spoke.

On an unusually low tide, Paws froze at the waterline near the cove and stared hard at nothing. He took two steps forward, halted again, and sneezed once—his "smell wrong" noise. There, half-buried under wrack and smooth black cobble, a narrow pipe the color of old bone poked from the sand, angled just so. No signage. No outfall number. At its mouth a pale foam breathed with the tide.

Mark knelt and tasted the air. Not sewage. Not oil. A sweet, chemical breath that made his molars ache a little.

"Document," Sarah said. She filmed from three angles, then took stills of the pipe, the foam, the line back to the bluff. Mark measured, then—carefully—took a water sample using a kit the county had trained them to use, the kind you shook like a potion and sealed like evidence.

"Back lot above this section is... what?" Sarah asked, already mapping.

"Warehouse," Mark said. "Small one. New roof. Old permits."

That night a black SUV idled at the end of their street for ten motionless minutes. No plate visible. No lights. When it finally rolled off, Paws followed it to the edge of the yard and watched it go, tail down but not tucked, chest out, ears up. He didn't bark. He watched.

They sent the sample to the county lab with a note flagged Priority: Unmarked Discharge. The report came back two days later with numbers and compounds that didn't belong in a cove: surfactants, a solvent that had no business near water, trace metals that looked like a machine's sweat.

Sharma and a county inspector stood above the cove three mornings later with clipboards and a warrant. They traced the line back to a clever, illegal tie-in: a floor drain hidden under a mat in a building whose business license described it as storage.

The fine was large. The cap went on. The SUV did not come back. The warehouse windows flickered with lights late the next night anyway—panic cleaning. Mark installed two more trail cams. Sophie learned what a solvent smells like and what wind brings to a nose that pays attention.

"Not everything is a cartoon villain," Sarah told her. "Most of the damage that matters is a person taking a shortcut because no one was watching. So we watch."

With attention came friction, the kind that made teeth grind. A coalition of beach businesses posted a letter calling the Guardians "well-intentioned but alarmist" and urging them to "balance environmental concerns with the needs of a tourism-driven economy."

Mark read it twice. "They mean don't scare customers," he said.

"We're not," Sarah said. "We're telling the truth and making it better."

They invited the coalition to a Lights Out pledge night anyway—no gotcha, no shame. They served lemonade and cheap cookies and asked for signatures on a simple card: dark during hatchings, ash cans full and emptied, a discount if a customer brings a reusable cup. Some owners signed with their whole bodies, grateful to be asked to do something bite-sized that mattered. A few refused and left early, taking their resentment with them like a coat worn in July.

One of them sent a scathing Facebook post that got three hundred likes and a dozen calls for the Guardians to "go home."

"This is home," Sophie typed, then deleted. She shut the app, leashed Paws, and walked the high line until the need to argue had burned itself to ash. Paws bumped her hand with his head and refused to let go until she laughed. He had a talent for pulling the plug on the part of anger that eats you.

The first fish kill came after a week of heat and a rain that hit like a dropped sheet of glass. The flood flashed off the roads, hit the warm shallows, and the cove went gray-green and then weird, then wrong—dozens of small fish rolling to the surface like coins in a trick you didn't want to see.

The smell crept. The calls started. By afternoon, county folks in waders waded and muttered words like deoxygenation and algal bloom and load.

The Guardians didn't argue science. They did what they could do: they flagged the worst pockets, set up a temporary barrier to keep kids out, and posted a calm, factual explainer on the hub: what this was, what causes it, what would make it happen less. That last bullet contained only three words: less dirty water.

At the emergency town hall, tension crackled like static. Beacon's liaison was there, aglow with contrition and rehearsal. Business owners were there, ragged with fear of a bad season. Sharma sat in the back with her arms folded, the expression of a woman who had done this before and would do it again.

Beacon's man slid into his pitch: partnerships, investments, "shared pathways forward." He did not say pipe, but every person in the room who had stood above the cove could smell it in his vowels.

Mark kept his remarks short, because anger was easy and accuracy was hard and nobody needed another speech that felt good and changed nothing. He spoke dollars and days and filters and fines that had worked. He pointed to the county engineer, who lifted a hand. It was boring in the best way—the boring of adults choosing to fix a thing.

Sarah had planned to sit quiet. Then a woman stood and blamed "activists" for "scaring families away with all this drama," and Sarah felt the calm, careful silence inside her crack. She walked to the mic.

"Children carried turtles to the ocean," she said, not raising her voice. "We pulled fishing line out of a bird's leg. We stuck a filter on an outfall. We picked up your cigarette butts when you couldn't be bothered. That's not drama. That's the work. If you want quiet, help us make a beach that doesn't need anyone to shout."

It was Sophie who made the room inhale. She didn't mean to speak. She did it because her legs carried her to the aisle and because Paws stood and went with her and because sometimes a child's plain sentence pierces a speech.

"We're not trying to ruin fun," she said, hand on Paws's head. "We're trying to keep the place we love alive. If you don't want to help, could you at least stop breaking it?"

There was a quiet, then a ripple of that particular sound communities make when they remember they are one.

The commission voted to fund the next two outfall filters. Beacon's liaison smiled, too smooth by half, and said how glad he was to be part of "real solutions."

Sharma caught Sarah and Mark on the steps after. "You have a target on you," she said, not ominous, just true. "So do I. It's fine. Just don't get tired of being careful."

"We're tired," Mark admitted. "We're not done."

"Good," she said. "See you Saturday. Gear Day III."

The weeks after were the kind that look like nothing in a novel and everything in a life: rebar tied with sunburnt fingers; a school visit where a kid asked what a *watershed* was and Sophie sketched a house, a hill, and an arrow in three strokes that made the whole room go "oh"; a note slipped under their door with a folded twenty and five words: For filters. Thank you all. They taped it to the fridge and put the twenty in the jar.

Golden Paws Day arrived whether they wanted the name or not. The council insisted and the kids loved it and, in the end, the Guardians let the banner fly because sometimes the smart choice is to accept a little corn with your community. There were booths with actual science and kid games that made more trash than they prevented until the kids redesigned them to be waste-free. There was an agility course Paws refused on principle and then completed at his own pace, pausing at the top of the A-frame to stare out at the line where the water met the sky and to thump his tail twice, as if to say yes, that.

A regional paper ran a story—*The Canine Guardian of Sunset Beach*—and for once the headline wasn't treacle. It talked about enforcement and filters and fines, about volunteers and data and civics, and also about a dog who had a nose for trouble and a knack for making people act better.

With attention came more visitors. With more visitors came careless trash and loud joy and money and eyes. The Guardians adjusted again: more ash cans, more signs in the language of teenagers, more patient conversations that could have been fights if anyone had arrived looking for one.

The work layered. The outfall at Harbor Lane stopped streaking rainbows. The illegal pipe at the cove stayed capped. The ATV tracks dwindled to the occasional rogue line that turned back at a freshly planted fence.

They lost small battles daily and won small ones just as often. The sum of it looked like nothing until you stepped back and realized the beach smelled clean more days than not.

Nights, when the house was finally quiet, Paws would lift his head and listen to a sound only he seemed to hear—a faint, intermittent hum offshore. He'd prick his ears, then decide it was nothing that needed his feet and lay his head back down with a sigh. Mark in the doorway would do the same.

But the hum kept coming. A sonar ping from a survey boat? A pump chugging after-hours on some distant barge? A new thing always arrives at the edge of the map sounding like a question.

On the last evening before school resumed, they walked to the cove again. The purple star-flowers in the driftwood crevice were gone, their seeds whisked off to try their luck elsewhere. The pipe's mouth sat clean, capped like a promise. At the bluff's base, someone had left a stack of smooth stones balanced impossible on impossible—a small sculpture of defiance against gravity and entropy.

"Who did that?" Leo asked.

"Somebody with steady hands," Mark said. "Somebody who wanted to leave something that says I was here without breaking anything."

Sophie set a shell on top—a white arc that caught the last light—and Paws tapped once with his nose, as if to approve the placement. Then he turned his gaze to the open water, where the horizon wore the day's last fire like a crown.

"You hear it?" Sophie whispered, hand on his ruff.

Paws tilted his head. He did. He always did.

"New semester," Sarah said, practical and hopeful. "New calendar. New projects. Same beach."

"Same dog," Leo said, burying his fingers in Paws's fur.

Mark looked out at the line where sea met sky and felt the familiar blend of relief and readiness that had become his equilibrium. The echoes of the waves were never just echoes. They were instructions, if you listened: come back, look close, start over, keep going.

They would. They had chosen this. The Guardians would keep the buckets stacked by the door, the red filters in the hall basket, the hemostats by the leashes, the hub's map dotted with pins like a constellation you learned by heart. They'd keep learning which fights needed voices and which needed hands and which needed three minutes at a podium with your best drawing.

And when the next hum grew into a shape, as hums always do, they would listen first. Paws would sit, and then he would stand, and then he would walk, and the rest of them—whole, tired, stubborn, in love with a piece of coast—would follow.

GLOSSARY

New Words You Learned in This Book

WORD	WHAT IT MEANS
Coastal Dune Ecosystems	The dynamic environments formed by sand dunes along coastlines, characterized by unique plant and animal communities adapted to sandy soil, wind, and salt spray.
Invasive Species	Non-native plants or animals that outcompete native species for resources, disrupting the ecological balance.
Native Species	Plants and animals that naturally occur in a specific region or ecosystem.
Nesting Sites	Areas where birds or other animals lay their eggs and raise their young, often requiring specific environmental conditions.
Stewardship	The responsible overseeing and protection of something considered worth caring for and preserving.
Untrammeled	Not restricted or confined; free.

www.ingramcontent.com/pod-product-compliance
Lightning Source LLC
Chambersburg PA
CBHW022044020426
42335CB00012B/538